D0442335

WHAT THE DOGS
HAVE TAUGHT ME

WHAT THE DOGS HAVE TAUGHT ME

And Other Amazing Things I've Learned

MERRILL MARKOE

Viking

VIKING
Published by the Penguin Group
Viking Penguin, a division of Penguin Books USA Inc.,
375 Hudson Street, New York, New York 10014, U.S.A.
Penguin Books Ltd, 27 Wrights Lane,
London W8 5TZ, England
Penguin Books Australia Ltd, Ringwood,
Victoria, Australia
Penguin Books Canada Ltd, 10 Alcorn Avenue, Suite 300,
Toronto, Ontario, Canada M4V 3B2
Penguin Books (N.Z.) Ltd, 182–190 Wairau Road,
Auckland 10, New Zealand

Penguin Books Ltd, Registered Offices:
Harmondsworth, Middlesex, England

First published in 1992 by Viking Penguin,
a division of Penguin Books USA Inc.

1 3 5 7 9 10 8 6 4 2

All the selections in this book first appeared in *New York Woman* with the exception of
"The Dog Diaries," which was first published in *Us* magazine, and "What the Dogs Have
Taught Me," which was originally published as the editor's foreword to *Late Night with
David Letterman: The Book*, edited by Merrill Markoe, Villard Books, copyright © 1985
by Cardboard Shoe, Inc., reprinted by permission of Villard Books, a division of Random
House, Inc. "A Conversation with My Dogs," "Firing My Dog," and "Evolution of the
Species. Not." appear for the first time in this collection.

LIBRARY OF CONGRESS CATALOGING IN PUBLICATION DATA
Markoe, Merrill.
What the dogs have taught me: and other amazing things I've learned /
Merrill Markoe.
p.   cm.
ISBN 0-670-84310-5
1. Dogs—Humor. I. Title.
PN6231.D68M35   1992
814'.54—dc20   91-39887

Printed in the United States of America
Set in Bodoni Book
DESIGNED BY JESSICA SHATAN
Illustrations by Bill Neeper

For Ronny and Gerry and Glenn . . .
and for Bob and Stan and Lewis

*I'd like to thank Dawn Drzal
and Helen Rogan for all their help,
and everyone else who was no help whatsoever.*

CONTENTS

A Conversation with My Dogs · 1

Look Before You Eat · 7

Tell Me Something Good · 13

Sexual Secrets and Other Self-Improvements · 19

The Markoe Plan for Overcoming Boredom
at a Baseball Game · 29

The Dog Diaries · 37

Creeping Gabor Syndrome · 45

Stupid Women, Stupid Choices · 53

Ah, Malibu! · 59

The Wacky World of Men · 65

Bob the Dog (1974–1988) · 71

Limo to Hell · 79

Viva Las Wine Goddesses! · 87

An Insider's Guide to the American Woman · 95

My Career in Stun Guns · 103

···················

Contents

Showering with Your Dog · 111

Markoe vs. *The Stars* · 119

Me and the Girls · 125

Write Like a Man · 131

12,000 Square Feet of Fun · 139

A Dog Is a Dog Is a Dog · 145

The Day I Turned Sarcastic · 151

Queen for a Day · 159

Home Alone · 165

I, Lewis · 171

House Pitiful · 177

Born Yesterday · 183

The Naked Truth · 191

Firing My Dog · 197

A World Without Men · 201

Conversation Piece · 207

Madonna and Carrie vs. Merrill and Elayne · 215

Evolution of the Species. Not. · 223

What the Dogs Have Taught Me · 231

· ·

WHAT THE DOGS
HAVE TAUGHT ME

A CONVERSATION WITH
MY DOGS

It is late afternoon. Seated at my desk, I call for my dogs to join me in my office. They do.

Me: The reason I've summoned you here today is I really think we should talk about something.

Bob: What's that?

Me: Well, please don't take this the wrong way, but I get the feeling you guys think you *have* to follow me *everywhere* and I just want you both to know that you don't.

Stan: Where would you get a feeling like that?

Me: I get it from the fact that the both of you follow me *everywhere* all day long. Like for instance, this morning. We were all together in the bedroom? Why do you both look blank? Doesn't this ring a bell at all? I was on the bed reading the paper . . .

Bob: Where was I?

Me: On the floor sleeping.

Bob: On the floor sleepi . . . ? Oh, yes. Right. I remember that. Go on.

Me: So, there came a point where I had to get up and go into the next room to get a Kleenex. And you *both* woke up out of a deep sleep to go with me.

Stan: Yes. So? What's the problem?

Bob: We *like* to watch you get Kleenex. We happen to think it's something you do very well.

Me: The point I'm trying to make is why do you both have to get up out of a deep sleep to go *with* me. You sit there staring at me, all excited, like you think something really good is going to happen. I feel a lot of pressure to be more entertaining.

Bob: Would it help if we stood?

Stan: I think what the lady is saying is that where Kleenex retrieval is concerned, she'd just as soon we not make the trip.

Bob: Is that true?

Me: Yes. It is.

Bob (deeply hurt): Oh, man.

Stan: Don't let her get to you, buddy.

Bob: I know I shouldn't. But it all comes as such a shock.

Me: I think you may be taking this wrong. It's not that I don't like your company. It's just that I see no reason for you both to follow me every time I get up.

Bob: What if just one of us goes?

Stan: And I don't suppose that "one of us" would be *you*?

Me: Neither of you needs to go.

Bob: Okay. Fine. No problem. Get your damn Kleenex alone from now on.

A Conversation with My Dogs

Me: Good.

Bob: I'm just curious. What's your position on pens?

Me: Pens?

Bob: Yes. How many of us can wake up out of a deep sleep to watch you look for a pen?

Me: Why would *either* of you want to wake up out of a deep sleep to follow me around while I'm looking for a pen?

Stan: Is she serious?

Bob: I can't tell. She has such a weird sense of humor.

Me: Let's just level with each other, okay? The *real* reason you both follow me every place I go is that you secretly believe there might be food involved. Isn't that true? Isn't that the real reason for the show of enthusiasm?

Stan: Very nice talk.

Bob: The woman has got some mouth on her.

Me: You mean you *deny* that every time you follow me out of the room it's actually because you think we're stopping for snacks?

Bob: Absolutely false. That is a bald-faced lie. We do it for the life experience. Period.

Stan: And sometimes I think it might work into a game of ball.

Bob: But we certainly don't *expect* anything.

Stan: We're *way* past expecting anything of you. We wouldn't want you to overexert yourself in any way. You have to rest and save up all your strength for all that Kleenex fetching.

Bob: Plus we know it doesn't concern you in the least that we're both *starving to death*.

Stan: We consume on the average about a third of the calories eaten daily by the typical wasted South American street dog.

Me: One bowl of food a day is what the *vet* said I should give you. No more.

Bob: One bowl of food is a joke. It's an hors d'oeuvre. It does nothing but whet my appetite.

Me: Last summer, before I cut your food down, you were the size and shape of a hassock.

Bob: Who is she talking to?

Stan: You, pal. You looked like a beanbag chair, buddy.

Bob: But it was not from overeating. In summer, I retain fluids, that's all. I was in very good shape.

Stan: For a hippo. I saw you play ball back then. Nice energy. For a dead guy.

Bob: Don't talk to me about energy. Who singlehandedly ate his way through the back fence. Not just once but on *four separate occasions?*

Me: So *you're* the one who did that?

Bob: One who did what?

Me: Ate through the back fence.

Bob: Is there something wrong with the back fence? I have no idea what happened. Whoever said that is a liar.

Stan: The fact remains that we are starving all day long and you continually torture us by eating right in front of us.

Bob: Very nice manners, by the way.

Me: You have the nerve to discuss my manners? Who drinks out of the toilet and then comes up and kisses me on the face?

Bob: That would be Dave.

Me: No. That would be *you*. And while we're on the subject of manners, who keeps trying to crawl *into* the refrigerator? Who always has *mud* on their tongue?

Stan: Well, that would be Dave.

Me: Okay. That *would* be Dave. But the point I'm trying to make is that where manners are concerned, let's just say that you don't catch me trying to stick my head in *your* dinner.

Bob: Well, that may be more a function of menu than anything else.

Me: Which brings me right back to my original point. The two of you do not have to wake up and offer me fake camaraderie now that you understand that *once* a day is all you're ever going to be fed. Period. Nonnegotiable. For the rest of your natural lives. And if I want to play ball, I'll say *so*. End of sentence.

Stan: Well, I see that the nature of these talks has completely broken down.

Bob: I gotta tell you, it hurts.

Me: There's no reason to have hurt feelings.

Stan: Fine. Whatever you say.

Bob: I just don't give a damn anymore. I'm beyond that, quite frankly. Get your own Kleenex, for all I care.

Stan: I feel the same way. Let her go get all the Kleenex and pens she wants. I couldn't care less.

Me: Excellent. Well, I hope we understand each other now.

Bob: We do. Why'd you get up? Where are you going?

Me: Into the next room.

Stan: Oh. Mm hmm. I see. And why is that?

Me: To get my purse.

Stan: Hey, fatso, out of my way.

Bob: Watch out, asshole. I was first.

Stan: The hell you were. *I* was first.

Bob: Fuck you. We're getting her purse, I go first. I'm *starving*.

Stan: You don't listen at all, do you. Going for *pens* means food. She said she's getting her *purse*. That means *ball*.

Look Before
You Eat

Only a woman under male surveillance will partake of quaint ceremonies like "dinnertime," featuring items from the major food groups arranged on a plate and served at a table. When a woman is alone and unobserved (and by *a woman* I of course mean me) she's likely to choose instead a supposedly calorie-conscious replacement for dinner: a couple of spoonfuls of yogurt at six o'clock, a few handfuls of dry shredded wheat or croutons at seven, a careful scanning of cupboards and refrigeration chambers at eight, followed by popcorn and pickle chips, wine or beers at ten and eventually a giant saucepan full of barely heated refried beans just before bed. I haven't calculated the overall caloric intake of this activity, but I suspect it's probably just about double what any ordinary sane meal might provide.

Which brings me to a topic in which I, as a single woman,

have achieved a certain unwilling expertise: eating out. This knowledge amounts to a short list of the particular signals that can tip you off to the inevitability of an overpriced, unsatisfying dining experience. I'm referring here to more subtle indicators than giant turquoise drinks garnished with parasols and served in ceramic whales—which actually can add a certain ironic hipness to the whole event that I find appealing. The following danger signals cannot serve in any ironic way whatsoever. Which is why I encourage you to memorize them as you would your social security number.

I. Signs Can Be Dangerous.

Exercise grave caution in the presence of any engraved wooden sign hanging outside the restaurant that uses words like "purveyors of" or "ye olde." The likelihood of anyone for miles around being from Merry Olde England is pretty slight. And stay away from any place that has a cute or excessively clever name—whether it involves a fictitious lovable curmudgeonly owner (like Señor Grumbley Wumbley or Dr. Munchies) or an adjective attached to an animal (like the Happy Hamster). This goes double for signs that show a cheery cartoon drawing of the animal dressed in a sailor suit dancing the hornpipe. Any restaurant that wants you to imagine your food having a great time on shore leave only moments before death does not deserve your patronage. Also to be avoided are restaurant names that suggest the food itself has a describable personality, like the Contented Carrot or the Good-Natured Potato. Maybe it's too obvious even to *mention* the n-apostrophe places, like Meat 'n' Wheat. But be afraid. Be very afraid.

II. Avoid Any Eating Establishment with a Visible Motif.

This means not only painted Grecian urns and fake antiquities, but lit torches, stagecoach parts, boat sections, pieces of driftwood, unattached wheels of all kinds, decorative remnants of air disasters, etc. I believe it is Newton's Third Law that tells us it's physically impossible for good food and fishnets full of glass balls to occupy the same space at the same time. Footnote: This particular rule applies only to places within a 100-mile radius of major metropolitan city limits. Once you have crossed that geographic barrier, it appears that decent family-style places can coexist quite nicely with out-of-season Christmas tree ornaments or preserved animal remains. Scientists are only now beginning to understand this phenomenon, so don't expect an explanation from me. Which leads directly to my next point, and perhaps my most puzzling:

III. A Place That Looks Like a Dump Doesn't Necessarily Serve Good Home Cooking.

All right. Having evaluated the exterior of the restaurant, it's time to step tentatively into the interior. We still have scrutinizing to do before we allow ourselves to be seated.

IV. If the Seating in the Restaurant Is Anything Other Than Tables, Chairs or Booths, Take a Hike.

Do not allow yourself to be seated on oldtime whiskey kegs, for example, or antique barrels or colorful containers of battery acid. Rattan peacock chairs, the kind that Huey P. Newton used to like being photographed in, are no exception to the rule, especially when accompanied by wooden ceiling fans or other Casablanca-style accessories.

V. Beware Too Much Wood.

Especially when it is pitched at a forty-five-degree angle. I can hear a lot of you resisting me on this one, claiming that wood provides a nice ambience. Be that as it may, it has been my experience that too much forty-five-degree angle wood reveals less about decor than it does about the presence of walleyed teenage chefs playing Space Invaders with frozen food packets and a microwave.

VI. Beware Multiple Dining Rooms.

Especially when accompanied by signs that say PARTY AND BANQUET FACILITIES or WE WELCOME TOUR BUSES. As a rule, anything (including blackened redfish) prepared in quantities of over 100 portions at once turns into Beefaroni.

VII. Beware No Other Customers.

This may not mean that you have stumbled upon a "find." The place has been found and then avoided by people with more sense than you will have if you stay.

VIII. Beware Colorful, Period-Style Uniforms.

"Olde English barmaids and wenches" are, of course, suspect, as are "cowpokes" and "pirates." And while the verdict's still out on "pouty European artistes," if you check with me in a year I will probably tell you that I always had a bad feeling about this ever-growing waitress motif.

....

At this point you may allow yourself to be seated, if you are not already so exhausted that you decide to give up. But do not place any sort of an order until you have carefully perused the menu for the following:

I. An Appropriate Degree of Menu-ness

By this is meant a piece of folded or laminated paper containing available meal selections and corresponding prices. The menu should not provide extra data about a historical period or culture that is supposed to trick you into thinking you are elsewhere. And it shouldn't be written on a rowboat oar or a dressmaker's dummy or hand-lettered on somebody's bare chest. Open the menu and promptly leave if you observe any of the following:

II. Use of the Phrase "Our Famous" or Worse, "Our World-Famous"

As seen in "our world-famous cheesecake" or "our world-famous salad bar." They not only never are, they can give you such serious pause for thought about the state of world fame that you can disappear into a searing depression for several weeks.

III. Repeated Use of Colorful Descriptive Words Such as "Zesty" or "Hearty"

Or colorful substitute nouns such as "grog" or "munchies" or "savories" or "victuals" or "libations." Or poetic renamings of the bland, as in "toast medley" or "vegetarian symphony."

IV. Mixture of Cuisines That Makes No Sense

A new Mexican restaurant opened up in what I laughingly call my neighborhood. It serves quesadillas with pine nuts and goat cheese. It's the rare kitchen staff that knows how to cook *one* cuisine very well, let alone CUBAN FOOD AND MANDARIN CHINESE. Remember, you're safest where they have fewer things to screw up.

V. Any Menu That Indicates I Had Any Hand in the Food Preparations

This includes any invitation to dinner at my house. I don't want to be too specific, but I have had warnings from the Board of Health and am one of the few private citizens whose kitchen has been closed by law.

Well, there you have it. *Bon appétit.* You're on your own.

Tell Me
Something Good

I have sampled many of L.A.'s rich fabric of 900 numbers. I'm not necessarily proud of this. It's just that they serve as a pretty good momentary distraction from having to write.

At least I haven't called all of them. I draw the line at phone sex, dating services and party lines. But I've listened to UFO updates (and learned we're hot on the trail of the first half-human, half-extraterrestrial baby). I've had a telephone tarot-card reading (hard to get excited once you realize the cards are being picked for you by a prerecorded voice). I've also tried some celeb hotline numbers, among them the two Coreys (Haim and Feldman), Tiffany and the New Kids on the Block, whose message answered the fascinating question "What is it like to do a celebrity photo shoot?" with the fascinating answer "Very glamorous, very glamorous."

If these 900 numbers could be rated as units of entertainment, I would formerly have placed them at the bottom of the list, between "a visit from the Jehovah's Witnesses" and "cleaning up after your dog." Then I discovered the one to which I developed a full-blown addiction. I speak, with some remorse, of Love Stars.

It works like this: You punch in your birthday. (See, it's not a general reading. It's about *you!*) You can hear "what the stars have to say about love in your life." You can get today's forecast, or any day in the past or future, or you can punch in the birthday of "that someone special" and get *both* your readings. If ever a concept appealed to the overheated thirteen-year-old in me, this was it.

On my first call, I entered my birthdate plus the birthdate of someone special.(And never you mind who it was. None of your beeswax.) Then I entered a date *in the past* so I could measure the prediction against real events. And when the cheery Brit who does the forecasting came through with a fairly accurate portrait, I was hooked. I began punching in birthdates and future dates in a touch-tone dialing frenzy.

It sort of occurred to me that this would probably add up to a larger phone bill than I'd be happy about, but I *just didn't care*. What's a little abstract anxiety compared with the concrete ecstasy I felt upon learning what the stars had to say about my love life? For instance, "Uranus is aspecting your Venus, bringing *an electric week of love* when you'll be hot and have your pick of various suitors. Your life is filled with pleasant surprises like late night visits or phone calls from admirers." Wow! Ain't I something? Or, "Mars is aspecting your Jupiter, bringing a time that is great for love and romance. You attract people like a magnet with your special glow, so get out! Look your best!" Suddenly, even if I spent my day totally alone, doing laundry and playing with hair gel, I was simultaneously leading the life I'd dreamed of. And the messages were specific—they meant *me*, Merrill Markoe, because the Love Stars people had factored in my birthday and everything. So what if I couldn't make any of their predictions actually materialize? This was certainly not their fault. They did their part—they *handed* me an electric week of love. That I couldn't live up to their expectations was my problem.

I was a Love Stars addict for at least a month, right up until the day that darned phone bill arrived. I'm too embarrassed to reveal the total (let me just hint that the calls cost about $3.45 apiece). Imagine my humiliation at seeing an endless repetition of the word *horoscope* down one side of the bill, a clear visual image of how far I had fallen (and, quite frankly, I don't know where I found the time to sit on the phone—as magnetic and electric as I was that month).

Another unforeseen consequence of calling Love Stars was the anger that every male friend of mine vented on me when I confessed this new hobby. Guys who considered me to be a woman of substance, not a helium-headed goofball, were more than disappointed. In fact, they were disgusted and repelled. "Merrill, for God's sake! You went to college!" railed George, a guy who likes to make odds and bet on a wide variety of sports events. "What *is* it about girls and this kind of crap?" my friend Harry snarled in disgust. Several successful women friends, however, wrote down the number, and *not one* of them said she thought less of me as a person.

Which brings me to yet another of my crackpot theories about the differences between men and women. Women seem to like the idea of fantastic forces that may control our destiny. In fact, I'd say that the entire clientele of Love Stars (assuming there *is* someone else besides me) is composed of females. It's surely no accident that there are horoscopes in *Vogue, Glamour, Mademoiselle, Woman, New Woman, Elle* and *Cosmo* . . . but not *Sports Illustrated, GQ, M, Esquire, Field & Stream* or *Guns & Ammo*. So why are women more drawn to the eerie mysteries of the great beyond than men?

Perhaps it is born of the same impulse that draws little girls to stories in which wishes are granted by magic, unlike little boys, who prefer fantasies of oversize vehicles equipped with capabilities for destruction. All the women I know who indulge do it because the end result is some assurance that things are going to be okay. Maybe our role as society's cheerleaders—the constant bolsterers of saggy male egos and needy children—leaves us wanting some kind of reassurance system ourselves. I know *I* enjoy a source of optimism, even if it's irrational. Or maybe it's the early conditioning (even if we as adults know better now) that trains girls to be passive. Psychic predictions are permission to be as passive as you want. My friend George postulated that guys want to *act* in their fantasies, rather than have them bestowed by unseen forces. He also feels that men would rather get something concrete for their fifty bucks—like a torque wrench or a glue gun.

TELL ME SOMETHING GOOD

Whatever the damn reason, this is a piece of bad behavior that I'd like to leave behind. So, having confessed publicly to these embarrassing foibles, I am going to say good-bye to my hocus-pocus years. I'll take it one day at a time—like they tell you at AA. I just wish there was a twelve-step program to help a person get off Love Stars. It's going to be tough saying good-bye to those electric weeks of love. Like today. The sun is aspecting my Neptune, meaning I'm due for "a romantic dream come true." I'm "hypnotic and erotic." "Intrigue and romance are coming my way." This is the sort of thing that's hard to walk away from.

SEXUAL SECRETS AND
OTHER SELF-IMPROVEMENTS

Here's something that New York and Los Angeles have in common that hardly ever makes the comparison charts: both have big piles of free extension-school course schedules sitting out on streets and in stores everywhere. I have been grabbing them for years now, simply for the pleasure of taking them home and saying in animated tones to myself, *Who attends these things?*

For example: "Writing Erotica: Sizzle Sells." Who the hell shows up at that one? And what do they even *mean* by teaching a course called "Charisma: How to Achieve That Special Magic"? So I thought I'd find out. I turned down "Learn About Your Season Through Color" and "Start Your Own Cooking Business . . . Now!" in favor of a couple that looked even more intriguing. As luck would have it, I turned up at part two of each course.

WHAT THE DOGS HAVE TAUGHT ME

I. "Sexual Secrets of the Orient"

As I walk up a flight of stairs in the lobby of a large hotel near the Los Angeles International Airport I can't help viewing everyone else headed up the stairs with suspicion. Are they here for the sexual secrets, too, and if so, why? Are they dangerous? Which is why, when I meet the instructor (in a meeting room full of rows of gold oval-backed hotel chairs), I am surprised. She is a short, stocky woman with no-nonsense graying hair and large earrings. She speaks with the deliberate manner of a grade school teacher, and she insists on giving me a name tag. "I don't want you to be just a no one," she tells me, not realizing that I am not the type to want a high-profile image at a class called "Sexual Secrets of the Orient."

Slowly the other class members are filtering in . . . and they are a pleasant-looking group of mostly white adults between the ages of twenty-five and forty-five—about half men and half women. There's a guy in a loud sport coat who looks like Dabney Coleman, two couples who look like Esalen Institute graduates, four cute guys in their twenties who seem to have come by themselves, and the regulation number of perky single women.

The instructor, whose name is Ginny Dingman and who is an R.N. with some degrees in Human Sexuality, begins to grill the assembled group. "Did you all write a sexual fantasy this week? Yes? No? *Please* remember to do that *this* week because it really gets the sexual energies flowing. What about drawing a picture of yourselves? Did you all look at yourselves in the mirror like you were supposed to?"

SEXUAL SECRETS AND OTHER SELF-IMPROVEMENTS

She suggests to us that women in the class might like to develop a nickname for their sexual organs. "The guys sometimes have names for their dick or their peter," she tells us, "so you can have a name, too. Like maybe Matilda. Or Melissa." She pushes her glasses up into her hair and walks up and down the aisle. "How many of you played with yourself this week? I want you to make a contract with yourself that you're going to play with yourself two to three times a week. Come on, guys! You laid cold hard cash down!" As she distributes our first handout I am thinking to myself that these secrets of the Orient are a lot more accessible than I had figured. Now we read about the pubococcygeal muscle, which, she tells us, is used to start and stop the flow of urine. "I'll call it the Kegel muscle, and I want you to start becoming a Kegel muscle exerciser on the freeway with me. I am working my Kegel muscle right now, as I talk to you. And when I get stuck in freeway traffic I just sit there going Kegel, Kegel, Kegel, Kegel, Kegel."

As cute as she is (and she is cute), she does have a compulsion to tell the class more personal information than I have ever really wanted to know about one of my teachers. We learn that she is fifty-seven and has a fifty-nine-year-old husband who has no erectile problems, that she was a bed wetter until she was sixteen and never had an orgasm until she was forty-eight, that it takes her a long time to lubricate, that she was once in a car wreck that gave her horrible intestinal problems and constipation for a time, and that she and her husband did drawings of their sexual organs that now hang proudly in the bathroom of their home. The class is a one-woman tour de force for Ginny, who, at other points during the evening, massages one guy's back, one woman's leg and another woman's butt, walks around the room touching everyone with a vibrator, shows us how to bounce testicles in our hands, demonstrates a palms-on-the-nipples massage technique on her own ample breasts and previews for us a wealth of unusual poems and reading materials, including but not limited to "the cunt coloring book."

Things do take a turn for the slightly more Oriental as we move on to the semi-exotic Ben Wa balls. "When I first started wearing these I had had four babies and three abdominal surgeries," Ginny says, holding a set up, "and I had no muscle tone in there. And they'd fall right out. I was the goose that laid the golden eggs." Ben Wa balls, she tells us, were developed by Oriental women to strengthen the Kegel muscle. "So what happens is they roll around and go doodledy-doodledy-doo." "What do they feel like?" a woman in the class wants to know. "Thank you very much for asking that," says Ginny, who explains that during intercourse men find them pleasurable but women report it doesn't feel that great. "Is there any way they can be pushed in so you can't get them out?" asks another woman. "Oh gosh, you ask wonderful questions!" says Ginny, who counsels us that if they do get lost, "just take a bath. Wash the dishes. Don't worry. They'll come out."

During the break I talk to a thin, waiflike blond woman who says she prefers being called Ocean (although her name tag reads AGNES). She tells me she is a private tutor in reading improvement, vocabulary building and intellectual enrichment who is taking the class to aid in her quest to become a "four-star A-double-plus lover," because she believes that "being a disciple of Aphrodite is one of the best uses of your time while you're here on Earth."

The cute guy with the beard who is sitting in front of me turns out to be a business-machine repairman who came here from Russia seven years ago. He doesn't think they had any similar classes in the Soviet Union, but he does feel he picked up some useful tips here tonight. He has previously enrolled in Windsurfing and hiking classes.

As it turns out, there are many repeat offenders among course graduates. The blond woman in front (who appears to be with her girlfriend) says she has also taken "Letting Go and Moving On" and "Direct Mail: The Marketing Phenomenon of the Decade."

"Thanks a lot, guys. We did it!" are Ginny's parting words to us, at about 10 P.M. And off into the night walk twenty-five strangers, all bearing sexual secrets.

II. "Looking for Someone: A Career as a Private Detective"

The description in the book said, "Learn surveillance, interview, interrogation and undercover techniques."

The class is being held at the Nick Harris Detective Academy, which turns out to be a small brick building in the San Fernando Valley. There, inside a regulation-style classroom, a small wiry-haired man named Milo Speriglio is standing at a podium. Despite the fact that there are only fourteen people attending tonight, he is addressing the class with a microphone. A plaque attached to the front of the podium says NICK HARRIS DETECTIVE AGENCY. SINCE 1911. Against the back wall of the classroom is a giant banner that reads NICK HARRIS DETECTIVE AGENCY. SINCE 1907. I am a couple of minutes late arriving so I sneak to an empty desk; on it is an "information kit," the front page of which says NICK HARRIS DETECTIVES. FOUNDED IN 1906. But never mind. Milo correctly identifies me as the woman who is coming from a magazine. "What magazine are you with?" he asks me. "*New York Woman*," I answer. "Oh," he says, "I didn't know it was a woman's magazine. Is it M-r-s or M-s or M-i-s-s? I was once interviewed by Gloria Steinberg." "No," I tell him, "it's called *New York Woman* magazine." "Does it have anything to do with *Playboy* or *Playgirl*?" he asks me. I can see a pack of Kool cigarettes through the pocket of his translucent yellow shirt. On each of his wrists is a crushed-gold wristband: one watch, one bracelet. He is also wearing several rings. Now Milo holds up a pen. "Anyone know what this is?" he asks. No one is dumb enough to say "a pen." Someone says, "A transmitter?" "It has been determined that Marilyn Monroe was murdered," Milo answers, "and using my magic pen—I just touch the top of it—" He does so and activates an audiotape of some interviews he conducted during his apparently endless investigation of this case. For the next fifteen or twenty minutes we listen to a man he calls his "deep throat" and another guy, who says one of his ambulances drove Monroe's body. He gives more obscure information than I ever wanted about this particular incident. "Was she staring to turn blue?" Milo asks the ambulance guy. "Well, the patient would inevitably turn blue, yes" is part of what I hear before I begin to tune it all out. A blond woman in the next row is picking hairs off her giant shoulder pads. The class is predominantly female: eleven women in summerwear and three men who look considerably grungier. When the tape is over, Milo asks for questions and someone asks for more information about "pretext," a concept that was apparently introduced last week, at the first part of this course. Milo says he *might* give additional examples were it not for the presence of a certain magazine reporter.

Milo now entertains us with anecdotes regarding his own wacky escapades . . . like the time he made an illegal U-turn on Sunset Boulevard: "I'm being chased and so I take out my credentials . . . which look very close to that of another investigative bureau—I forgot the name of it but the initials are FBI. . . ."

"Any more questions?" A thirtyish man in a Mickey Mouse T-shirt shoots up his hand. During an upcoming break I learn that his name is Jim and that he is a plumber from Pomona. Jim thinks that being a private detective might be a more interesting job, "for a while anyway." (No newcomer to the world of extension programs, Jim last attended a course in "Makeup and Skin Care," where he learned to "drink lots of water and use certain creams and stuff like that.") Now he wants to know if some detectives use multiple identities. "Yes," says Milo, "when they're using subterfuge or pretext. They won't come out and say, 'I'm John Smith.' They might say, 'I'm *Jack* Smith' or something like that."

As the class goes on, Jim has a great many questions to ask. He wants to know if hypnosis can help you beat a lie detector. He wants to know if you can file your fingerprints off or whether the application of glue will cause them to disappear. He wants to know whether galoshes will eliminate footprints. I begin to wonder, *Why exactly does he want to know?*

Now Fawn wants to know if Milo has worked on "cases of international proportions." She is wearing a ponytail pulled to one side of her head. Just this week she got dumped from her job in sales, and, she tells me, she has enrolled as a full-time student here. "Yes," says Milo. "Can you give some examples?" she asks. "No," he says, eliciting light laughter. I talk to the hennaed woman with braces and checkerboard socks who is seated behind me. She is Candy, a woman who has taught grade school for seventeen years, but thinks that someday she might like to have another career. Now she feels she wouldn't really want to be a private detective because she doesn't really like the idea of using pretense in dealing with people.

Before the class ends Milo shows us how to write on money with a crayon that can only be seen in ultraviolet light, and demonstrates equipment that makes a beep when it gets near hidden bugs or wiretaps. I realize I have been regularly checking my watch to see how late it is getting, pretty much the way I used to do when I was in high school. On my way out I chat with a stocky fiftyish woman named Judy Johnston, who tells me she just retired from her job as an accounts-payable clerk. Judy looks as unlikely a candidate for a career as a private detective as any living creature has a right to. But she tells me she has always been interested in the field. And so she was disappointed. "I felt we didn't really learn a whole lot. I feel like I paid forty dollars for very little. But I'm interested in taking the investigator course," she says as she unlocks her car.

What I Have Learned from My Studies

1. FBI agents bend their car antennae so they will recognize each other.

2. Woman-on-top and rear-entry-knees-to-chest are the best positions for getting hit in the G-spot.

3. It's easiest to take criminal fingerprints off a dead body.

4. Four women that Ginny Dingman knows set off airport metal detectors by trying to go through wearing Ben Wa balls.

5. The most dangerous form of private-eye work is process serving.

6. There is an Oriental sexual practice in which you take a silk string with knots in it and insert it up your lover's rectum. At the moment of orgasm you slowly pull it out. The key word here is *slowly*, for you can pull out a person's intestinal tract, which, for people like me, is really a giant turnoff. In fact, I'm not sure that some of these darn sexual secrets weren't better off when they were secrets.

THE MARKOE PLAN
FOR OVERCOMING BOREDOM
AT A BASEBALL GAME

*Now that the baseball season is finally danc-*ing gaily to a close, I can say it: I am not really a sports fan. I'm ashamed to admit it—in fact, I'm so ashamed that I added the word *really* to the previous sentence to make it sound as if I'm on the fence about the whole thing. I only wish I were.

I feel as intensely embarrassed about this as I do about my love for oversize, parasol-laden tropical cocktails in primary colors, with names that have a noun and more than one adjective or adverb. And I know I should be different. These are exactly the kinds of female stereotypes that I'd like to be able to sidestep. But now, after several decades of giving it the old college try (usually in the name of love), I am beginning to abandon hope.

Over the years I have attended a wide variety of sports

events and logged countless hours in front of televised versions of same—each time hoping that *this* will be the magical moment when the veil lifts and I will be able to detect exactly what it is that I am supposed to relate to emotionally. But no payoff.

So why does this whole thing still concern me, you ask? Because it has become increasingly obvious that most appealing men are fanatical about at least one ball sport. And it becomes necessary for a woman who wishes to be with such men to develop, as I have, a reasonable strategy for survival. Since I trust I am not the only person still struggling with this, I offer you:

The Markoe Plan for Overcoming Boredom at a Baseball Game

1. SNACKS. Eating and drinking play an important part in this survival strategy. You will want to make many, many trips to the various snack bars. Think of your visit to the stadium as a stop at a giant open-air cafeteria that has a really awful ambience. People are shouting, there is a continuous selection of terrible short songs on the electric organ, and the menu is very limited (to say nothing of the wine list). Which is why I advise you to try a twenty-four-hour fast before attending any game. This gives you permission to indulge in the wide variety of poisonous meat and fried-dough snacks you might otherwise avoid. Be sure to buy at least one of everything and exercise your every condiment option. Tempting indigestion is just one more way to keep yourself awake and amused.

Overcoming Boredom at a Baseball Game

I personally recommend a hearty consumption of beer, but for those of you who usually abstain, an alternate beverage will do. The resulting trips to the rest room will be a welcome distraction and the best aerobic exercise available under the circumstances.

2. SHOPPING. Souvenirs at a ball game can be a real disappointment to any seasoned shopper because most of the clothing items are 100 percent polyester. And, let's face it, those dolls with the spring-loaded heads are depressing, even to tiny children. Nevertheless, this remains one of your few viable diversions, so inspect each item carefully. And, for extra fun, ask the salesperson if he or she can give you any information about the Korean or Taiwanese villages where these items were manufactured. The resulting reactions will look like moments in a David Lynch film, so bring your camera.

3. LOOKING FOR CUTE GUYS. As soon as you enter the ballpark, be sure to purchase a program. This will enable you to begin your game-long search for cute guys. When you spot one, memorize his name and number. Now you're all set to follow him, not just in today's game, but in life, as he travels the traditional road from sociopathic relationships to nasty paternity or palimony suits, and then on through assorted felonies and underwear modeling.

4. A DANGEROUS SEAT. Since it may not have been your idea to attend the game in the first place, you probably won't be consulted about seating. But if you do have any influence, request a seat between home plate and first base. Here you will encounter a steady flow of popup and fly balls as they rain down upon the spectators. This works to your benefit because nothing can keep a dulled brain fresh and alert like the very real threat of a broken face.

5. CONVERSATION. Something is called for during those long stretches of time when you have nothing relevant to say and you have wisely decided not to embark on a discussion of your relationship. So memorize the following question and ask it with an air of quizzical bemusement: "Honey, what was the difference between the batting average and the slugging average again?" Now sit back, relax, eat, start an art project or even take a nap—there will not be another conversational lull for hours and hours.

6. SELF-HYPNOSIS. Perhaps you're at a point in the game where you have eaten a lot and drunk a lot and maybe even purchased some cheap souvenirs. You look up and realize that you still have six innings to go. What to do? Well, this is where the simple technique of self-hypnosis can become your friend.

Start by imagining that you are on a beautiful island in the Caribbean, the sun caressing your dewy skin, a warm breeze blowing peacefully through your mane of golden-yellow hair. Now consider how much this is costing you. Not just hotel bills, airfares and eating out, but new swimwear, new evening wear and the money it cost to bleach your hair golden-yellow. Next, remember that you are flirting with skin cancer and premature aging. Realize that this is *not paradise but a nightmare*, and then, gently, gently, bring yourself back to the wonderful stadium, where the worst thing that can happen to you is that you will have to stay until the very end of the ninth inning. You are a very, very lucky girl, and I think you know it.

7. DEVELOP TEAM LOYALTY. This may be the best answer to your problems, since it is considered reasonable to have a maniacal devotion to one team. And there is no better choice, year in, year out, than the Cubs, because they usually get eliminated early in the season. This legitimizes your desire to pay only minimal attention. "I'm just not into it anymore this year," you say ruefully. "Not since the Cubs got beat." Believe it or not, everyone will understand and respect you, even offer you sympathy.

Ideally, the responsibility for keeping the non-fan amused would be shared voluntarily by the concerned fan. And so, on the remote chance that the current Mideast turbulence makes people treasure their loved ones with renewed enthusiasm, I offer the fan some suggestions for helping the non-fan stay alert and cheerful.

1. POINT OUT TAWDRY PERSONAL DETAILS. Regale your foggy friend with sleazy tales of Steve Garvey, Wade Boggs, Pete Rose, Jose Canseco, *et al.* Number 18 suddenly becomes a lot more interesting to the non-fan if he turns out to be the guy whose girlfriend was on Oprah because she is suing him.

2. SECRET MESSAGES. I don't know what kind of muscle it takes to pull a thing like this together, but if you could inform the non-fan that you've arranged for special messages to play amid the barrage of statistics on the Diamond Vision screen, I guarantee you will be sitting beside someone who is suddenly paying rapt attention, filled with an intoxicating mixture of excitement and nauseating anxiety as she waits to discover what endearing or hellish sentiment you have chosen to share with her and a stadium full of thousands of people.

3. SEVENTH-INNING STRETCH TREATS AND SURPRISES. Honoring the tradition of giving the non-fan something to look forward to, agree in advance that when everyone else gets up to sing "Take Me Out to the Ball Game," you will submit to a quality-time discussion of where the relationship is headed. (Come on. You know you don't really want to sing "Take Me Out to the Ball Game" anyway.) Add to that a spontaneous presentation of lovely gift items, and there's no reason why the seventh-inning stretch can't be restructured into a miniature version of Valentine's Day. (There's no real reason why it can't be modified into a scaled-down version of Thanksgiving or Easter either, but let's just leave it at Valentine's Day for now, and, if it seems to go well, we'll see about adding other holidays later in the year.)

4. PERSONAL BETTING. I know this is strictly taboo and that players get tossed out of the game, etc., etc., for this sort of thing, but in my opinion there is no better way to keep a brain-dead female awake than by making the score a direct route to a better social or sexual life. I suggest bets along the lines of "If we lead by at least six in the bottom of the fourth, I'll let *you* pick what we do next weekend, and I won't whine even if it's a foreign film with subtitles."

OVERCOMING BOREDOM AT A BASEBALL GAME

Or, "If the Mets are winning by more than six points at the bottom of the seventh, I'll attend at least a month's worth of couple therapy. *And* I'll try to remember to initiate foreplay."

THE DOG DIARIES

I pick dogs that remind me of myself—
scrappy, mutt-faced, with a hint of mange. People look for
a reflection of their own personalities or the person they
dream of being in the eyes of an animal companion. That
is the reason I sometimes look into the face of my dog Stan
and see wistful sadness and existential angst, when all he
is actually doing is slowly scanning the ceiling for flies.

We pet owners demand a great deal from our pets. When
we give them the job, it's a career position. Pets are required
to listen to us blithely, even if we talk to them in infantile
and goofy tones of voice that we'd never dare use around
another human being for fear of being forced into psychiatric
observation. On top of that, we make them wear little sweat-
ers or jackets, and not just the cool kind with the push-up
sleeves, either, but weird little felt ones that say, *It's raining
cats and dogs*.

WHAT THE DOGS HAVE TAUGHT ME

We are pretty sure that we and our pets share the same reality, until one day we come home to find that our wistful, intelligent friend who reminds us of our better self has decided a good way to spend the day is to open a box of Brillo pads, unravel a few, distribute some throughout the house, and eat or wear all the rest. And we shake our heads in an inability to comprehend what went wrong here.

Is he bored or is he just out for revenge? He certainly can't be as stupid as this would indicate. In order to answer these questions more fully, I felt I needed some kind of new perspective, a perspective that comes from really knowing both sides of the story.

Thus, I made up my mind to live with my pets as one of them: to share their hopes, their fears, their squeaking vinyl lamb chops, their drinking space at the toilet.

What follows is the revealing, sometimes shocking, sometimes terrifying, sometimes really stupid diary that resulted.

8:45 A.M. We have been lying on our sides in the kitchen for almost an hour now. We started out in the bedroom with just our heads under the bed. But then one of us heard something, and we all ran to the back door. I think our quick response was rather effective because, although I never ascertained exactly what we heard to begin with, I also can't say I recall ever hearing it again.

9:00 A.M. We carefully inspected the molding in the hallway, which led us straight to the heating duct by the bedroom. Just a coincidence? None of us was really sure.

••••••••••••••••••••••••

So we watched it suspiciously for a while. Then we watched it for a little while longer.

Then, never letting it out of our sight, we all took a nap.

10:00 A.M. I don't really know whose idea it was to yank back the edge of the carpet and pull apart the carpet pad, but talk about a rousing good time! How strange that I could have lived in this house for all these years, and never before felt the fur of a carpet between my teeth. Or actually bit into a moist, chewy chunk of carpet padding. I will never again think of the carpet as simply a covering for the floor.

11:15 A.M. When we all wound up in the kitchen, the other two began to stare at me eagerly. Their meaning was clear. The pressure was on for me to produce snacks. They remembered the old me—the one with the prehensile thumb, the one who could open refrigerators and cabinets. I saw they didn't yet realize that today, I intended to live as their equal. But as they continued their staring, I soon became caught up in their obsession. That is the only explanation I have as to why I helped them topple over the garbage. At first I was nervous, watching the murky fluids soak into the floor. But the heady sense of acceptance I felt when we all dove headfirst into the can more than made up for my compromised sense of right and wrong. Pack etiquette demanded that I be the last in line. By the time I really got my head in there, the really good stuff was gone. But wait! I spied a tiny piece of tinfoil hidden in a giant clump of hair, and inside, a wad of previously chewed gum, lightly coated with sugar or salt. I was settling down to my treasure when I had the sense that I was being watched. Raising my head just slightly, I looked into the noses of my companions. Their eyes were glued to that hard rubber mass. Their drools were long and elastic, and so, succumbing to peer pressure, I split up my gum wad three ways. But I am not sure that I did the right thing. As is so often the case with wanting popularity, I may have gained their short-term acceptance. But I think that in the long run, I lost their real respect. No dog of reasonable intelligence would ever divide up something that could still be chewed.

11:50 A.M. Someone spotted a fly, and all three of us decided to catch him in our teeth. I was greatly relieved when one of the others got to him first.

12:20 P.M. Someone heard something, and in a flash, we were all in the backyard, running back and forth by the fence, periodically hooting. Then one of us spotted a larger-than-usual space between two of the fence boards, and using both teeth and nails, began to make the space larger. Pretty soon, all three of us were doing everything in our power to help. This was a case where the old prehensile thumb really came in handy. Grabbing hold of one of the splinters, I was able to enlarge the hole immediately. Ironically, I alone was unable to squeeze through to freedom, and so I watched with envy as the others ran in pointless circles in the lot next door. What was I going to do? All of my choices were difficult. Sure, I could go back into the house and get a hacksaw, or I could simply let myself out the back gate, but if I did that, did I not betray my companions? And would

I not then be obligated to round us all up and punish us? No, I was a collaborator, and I had the lip splinters to prove it. So I went back to the hole and continued chewing. Only a few hundred dollars' worth of fence damage later, I was able to squeeze through that darn hole myself.

1:30 P.M. The extra time I took was just enough for me to lose sight of my two companions. And so, for the first time, I had to rely on my keen, new animal instincts. Like the wild creature I had become, I was able to spot their tracks immediately. They led me in a series of ever-widening circles, then across the lot at a forty-five-degree angle, then into a series of zigzags, then back to the hole again. Finally, I decided to abandon the tracking and head out to the sidewalk. Seconds later, I spotted them both across the street, where they were racing up and back in front of the neighbor's house. They seemed glad to see me, and so I eagerly joined them in their project. The three of us had only been running and hooting for less than an hour when the apparent owner of the house came to the front door. And while I admit this may not have been the best of circumstances for a first introduction, nevertheless I still feel the manner in which he threatened to turn the hose on us was both excessively violent and unnecessarily vulgar.

Clearly, it was up to me to encourage our group to relocate, and I was shocked at how easily I could still take command of our unit. A simple "Let's go, boys," and everyone was willing to follow me home. (It's such a power-packed phrase. That's how I met my last boyfriend!)

3:00 P.M. By the time we had moved our running and

hooting activities into our own front yard, we were all getting a little tired. So we lay down on our sides on the porch.

4:10 P.M. We all changed sides.

4:45 P.M. We all changed sides again.

5:20 P.M. We all lay on our backs. (What a nice change of pace!)

6:00 P.M. Everyone was starting to grow restless. Occasionally, one of us would get up, scratch the front door, and moan. I wrestled silently with the temptation simply to let us all in. But then I realized I didn't have any keys on me. Of course, it occurred to me that we could all go back through the new hole in the fence, but everyone else seemed to have forgotten about the entire fence incident by this time. As they say, "a word to the wise." And so, taking a hint from my friends, I began to forget about the whole thing myself.

6:30 P.M. The sound of an approaching car as it pulls into the driveway. The man who shares this house with us is coming home. He is both surprised and perplexed to see us all out in the front yard running in circles. He is also quickly irritated by the fact that no one offers any explanations. And once he opens the front door, he unleashes a furious string of harsh words as he confronts the mounds of garbage someone has strewn all over the house. We have nothing but sympathy for him in his tragic misfortune. But since none of us knows anything about it, we all retire to the coat closet until the whole thing blows over. And later, as he eats his dinner, I sit quietly under the table. As I watch him, a pleasant feeling of calm overtakes me as I realize just how much I have grown as a person. Perhaps that is why the cruel things he says to me seem to have no effect. And so, when he gets up to pour himself another beverage, I raise my head up to his plate, and, with my teeth, I lift off his sandwich.

CREEPING GABOR
SYNDROME

The other day my answering machine broke, and the idea of having to live for even five minutes without being able to get my messages or screen my calls made me so panicky that I immediately reorganized my day around an emergency trip to buy another. Clearly I have become a southern California cliché. And now I feel compelled to reveal another, even darker terror I face on a daily basis. I think there is a chance I am turning into Zsa Zsa Gabor.

At first glance, our biographical profiles are not especially similar. She's been much married, and I, well, I've been much lived-togethered. She has a tiny, overly manicured dog with a pedigree, and I have a large bad-smelling mixed breed from the pound who has three extra toes on each of his feet. Zsa Zsa has always been for me a symbol of female excesses gone berserk: the hair, the gowns, the furs, the jewels, the makeup. We were, I always felt, polar opposite types of human female, so utterly different that one day a study at Johns Hopkins University might reveal that there were, in fact, *three* sexes: men, Zsa Zsa–women and Merrill-women. This was back before I noticed my behavior starting to change.

At first it was subtle, like in that movie *The Fly*. A couple of years ago I had some streaks put in my hair. This met with displeasure from my significant other, who looked at the results with one raised eyebrow and an expression that defrosted the refrigerator and said, "So! You are what exactly now? A strawberry blonde?" Embarrassed, I disavowed any knowledge of the whole thing, claiming to have been hypnotized by a hairdresser on crack. But the truth is I just wanted to try it.

As a folk singer–wannabe in high school I'd rejected any involvement with artificiality in grooming. I laughed in the face of hairstyles, makeup and accessories right on through college. I bought my clothes at Army surplus warehouses or thrift stores (the general dress code being combat wear for daytime, cast member of *The Madwoman of Chaillot* for evening).

Then after college I did some time in an unheated log cabin in the Sierra Nevada mountains, where I tried to sport a look that said, "If I wanted to, I could bake bread." (Luckily for all, no one challenged me to prove it.) And I just kept on looking that way until I joined the adult work force in L.A., which is when it dawned on me that certain things didn't look so cute after you turned thirty. Especially things that had seemed girlishly unself-conscious when I was a teenager—oversize clothes, say, or hair in your eyes and an adorable smudge on your face in the tradition of Goldie Hawn.

So I began, cautiously, to tiptoe around in the world of grooming, starting out with real haircuts from a real hairdresser (complete with stern admonishments that I'd better stop cutting my bangs with manicure scissors). Next I just sort of fell into purchasing an outfit, *with accessories*, forced down my throat by a very persuasive saleswoman. The effect garnered compliments, I noticed. And not long afterward I made a tiny foray into mascara and blusher.

At first I had to hide these items from my boyfriend, who was known to feel that makeup wearers were plastic and superficial. But, like most men, he was pretty naive. "You look very nice this evening," he'd say, peering at my face. "Were you out in the sun today?" Yeah. Right, pal. That's it. I was out in the sun, and I spent so much time out there it caused my eyelashes to stick straight out, too.

So life unfolded (as it is wont to do), and before long the boyfriend was dust in the wind and I was free to flaunt. In no time at all I was a licensed eyeliner owner, hurtling like a speeding train into eye shadow and lip gloss.

Of course there were setbacks. My next boyfriend didn't like makeup either. "Why do you have green stuff on your eyelids?" I remember him asking, with an expression that killed quite a few of my houseplants. "Why do I have what?" I stalled. "I have *green stuff on my eyelids?* Oh, my God, let me go check." I would run into the bathroom, quickly wipe it off and come out apologizing, claiming to have had some kind of mildew accident. If *he* didn't like it, then *I* didn't like it because, after all, women wear makeup to *attract* men, not *repel* them. But now he's a ghost, too, and I can be as repulsive as I want. I've still got the green stuff, plus some blue stuff, tan stuff, pink stuff and even some purple stuff.

My personal drift toward Gabor syndrome became more pronounced when I began to appear on television as a contributing reporter on a local newscast. Right before I sat down between the handsome anchorman and the cornball weatherman, I would report to the makeup room and watch as a makeup professional slathered me to the gills with *real* makeup.

"What are you doing?" I would ask, as she put white stuff around my eyes. "Gotta get rid of those dark circles," she replied, and so saying introduced me to the concepts of concealer and makeup base—and to the fact that I had dark circles. I'd spent the previous thirty-odd years unaware they existed, but now when I looked in the mirror they were all I could see. And so it came to pass that I learned about lip liner (liquid or pencil) and finishing powder . . . the whole enchilada. I could no longer claim naiveté. Now if I looked drab and boring it was my choice. Yes, I knew everything Zsa Zsa knew (except how to get booked on *Hollywood Squares*).

I had become a member of a prime demographic sample: women with checking accounts who know what is in those bottles at cosmetics counters. At first I was alarmed to learn I should be "exfoliating" my skin and wearing different

moisturizers for day and night, but before long I had my very own container of that-stuff-you-put-on-your-eyes-when-you-go-to-sleep. I had joined the ranks of southern Californians obsessed with skin care and grooming.

Which brings us to last Saturday, when I ran into my agent Bill in the cosmetics department at Neiman-Marcus. We were both stocking up on moisturizer. (If you want to know who my agent is, he's currently the *moistest* agent in L.A.) We met only a few yards from the spot where I was later relieved of several hundred dollars by a woman who was wearing five shades of eye shadow on each eyelid! I knew what was going to happen the minute I agreed to my "complimentary makeover plus a free $25 gift packet." I knew, and yet I was helpless to stop it.

That's how I found myself taking makeup advice from a woman who had five colors of eye shadow on each eyelid, while inches away, Beverly Hills men too old to be wearing powder-blue Levi's and white Reeboks prowled the makeup counters in the company of their much younger wives, all in pursuit of moister faces.

The woman who was redesigning me was also wearing three colors of lipstick. She selected Wild Melon Blush just for me, and the other women behind the counter nodded their approval. "You have a gorgeous face," one said, playing me like a violin, "but you need to heighten your features with *more color*." Ah, now I get it. More color. The other two ooohed and aaahed as Miss Eyelids showed me how to make myself look like a piñata.

Of course I wound up buying "just a few things" at a cost

of several hundred dollars. And when I finally got back outside to my car and checked the rearview mirror for a glimpse of my newly enhanced loveliness, I discovered that in daylight I looked like an aging hooker who had fallen asleep in the sun.

See, this is why I am worried. I *knew* it was a scam. I didn't even like how Miss Eyelids looked. Sitting in my car and trying to repair the damage with Kleenexes and saliva, I was thinking about how I'd *volunteered* for this and paid for it through the nose. Me! Merrill Markoe! The woman with the moistest agent in L.A.!

Then the next day when I was putting on my makeup I found myself thinking, "Hmmm. I wonder if one color of eyeshadow will be enough?" This is when the real fear hit me. I mean, since when is *five shades of eye shadow at once* a good idea? If someone told me that five pairs of shoes on one foot looked incredibly sexy, would I run out with a wheelbarrow to the shoe store? Hell, no! At least not until I first saw how it looked on Paulina Porizkova, and even then not until after I saw that it didn't look too bad on Diane Sawyer either and that the woman ahead of me in line at the market had on *three* pairs and looked kind of cool.

I tell myself that just because I own a lot of this stuff it doesn't mean I have to wear it. It doesn't mean that anything's really changed about me. Even though last week I suddenly felt compelled to paint my fingernails bright red for the first time in my life for no particular reason. After all, I'm still me: Merrill Markoe—the sensible eccentric girl who has the really moist agent. It doesn't mean I have to

eventually wind up in a mink stole with a head of that really big stiff white hair. Does it? Although I have been wondering how she gets it to stick out like that. Maybe I'll buy some sculpting gel and styling spray and experiment.

STUPID WOMEN, STUPID CHOICES

Put on alert by my foolproof "dumb-movie sensory system"—a highly developed sixth sense that reminds me to stay away from movies with titles containing numbers or accompanied by the words *produced by Simpson and Bruckheimer*—I had been purposely avoiding *Pretty Woman*. But *Pretty Woman* was the thing that wouldn't die. I kept seeing ads that called it "the feel-good hit of the season." And then it was rereleased so everyone would have a chance to see it *again*. And then came a barrage of new ads proclaiming that at long last the movie was available on videocassette.

Finally, I started to hear that ten-year-old girls were watching it over and over, and this was when I began to get concerned, because my own ten-year-old-girl fantasy fixations were the early starting point for a whole lot of trouble later on. So I gave in and saw the darn thing, and my short review is this: It really sucks and it pissed me off.

To recap briefly, the amazingly appealing Julia Roberts plays the most improbable hooker in the history of unlikely TV and movie hookers. She might as well have been portraying the Bean Goddess from Neptune, so unhookerlike is her character. (In fact, what we have here is the first true Disney hooker! The story could almost have been serialized on the old *Mickey Mouse Club* with Annette in the starring role!)

Anyway, here's the hooker dressed like Rocker Barbie, leading a life just a tad less brutal, alienating or problematic than that of any cosmetics counter saleswoman when she encounters repressed, handsome, egomaniac john Richard Gere. This man has just been dumped by his girlfriend because, she says, she is "sick of being at his beck and call." So he decides to hire this (wink, wink) *hooker* to be his temporary social companion. And as it turns out, not only does she not have any kind of a "beck and call" problem, something about this situation causes her to blossom, flower and *thrive!* Even though he never offers her anything in the way of emotional interaction, that doesn't affect her *incredible joie de vivre!* Because she's just so darned full of this drug-free, childlike wonderment at life! Wow! A hotel lobby! Yikes! Room service! A hat! A dress! A *really big* bathtub! Oh, my God! Pinch me! I'm dreaming!

Because this is a movie, she pretty soon falls in love with this guy. And now, when he offers to *pay* her to stay, she is hurt and packs up to leave. "It's just not good enough anymore," she says to him. "I want *the whole fairy tale!!*"

(And I'm thinking to myself, *Excuse me, but where was I when they rewrote the fairy tale to start, "Once upon a time, in a land far, far away, there was this hooker . . ."?*)

Anyway, these are the easy, lighthearted reasons to hate the movie. That it is evil and loathsome to glorify hooking and sociopathic men is kind of obvious. But the ending was the final straw. Moved to the kind of white-knight behavior that I have never seen exhibited, even in the name of love, by a human male of any race, creed or religion anywhere except in a movie, the Richard Gere character shows up at the last minute to *rescue* Julia Roberts and bring us to the super-disgusting last line. As he lifts her into his arms, she says, "And now I'll rescue you right back."

That was when the uncontrollable barfing started for me. Because I knew that the guys who made this movie were all patting themselves on the back, thinking that the line added some kind of Nineties contemporary woman's egalitarian spin to the proceedings. I really got revved up, thinking about the insanity of that mainstay of Hollywood romantic plot devices: *rescuing*.

(You: "Gee, Merrill is certainly very grumpy today. I wonder if she's getting enough potassium and magnesium.")

It's certainly a time-honored tradition to have women be the *rescued* party. (Cinderella and Sleeping Beauty spring to mind.) But the fantasies that had the tightest hold on me involved the woman as the *rescuer*. In my preteen years I went repeatedly to see *West Side Story* because I had the hots for all the (wink, wink) teenage gang members. They were the first versions of a fantasy prototype that I have always found a real winner—I speak of the wounded, brood-

ing, tough-guy loner with the mysterious tragic past, running, ever running, from unjust circumstances, his sad eyes the only clue to the horrible lack of love that has driven him to unfortunate acts of rage, rebellion and self-destruction. Now he is hurt, and dangerous to everyone except that one woman whose love might make a difference. It is she he can come to in the middle of the night as he hides from the "authorities" who have wronged him. Together they will walk through the turbulent weather, joint observers of life's cruelties, until he kisses her with such ferocity that she has no choice but to devote her very being to trying to save him.

Various versions of this scenario accompanied me through my girlhood in the form of James Dean, Clint Eastwood or even the young Bob Dylan; then, more recently, Sean Penn, Gary Oldman or Johnny Depp. (Girlhood nothing; I was mesmerized *last weekend* by the several male cast members who have been doing this dance on *Twin Peaks*.) And that got me to thinking, *Who are these guys playing? Who are these wounded, brooding guys in real life?* Finally, I realized that wounded, brooding loners in real life are the emotionally crippled, paranoid, narcissistic guys with drug and alcohol and commitment problems who drove the woman of the Eighties into a frenzy, writing, reading and buying that endless series of bestselling books with the long, annoying titles. I refer, of course, to the *Men Who Hate Women and the Women Who Love Them*, etc., genre.

Just about all these books are devoted to the premise that rescuing is not only futile, it is *impossible* (because someone can rescue himself, but no one can rescue another person).

These books contain chapter after chapter of advice on how to rebuild your decimated life and your shattered self-esteem—just two of the cute little by-products of your full-out rescuing attempt. In fact, in the past decade we have become a nation of Twelve-Step Programs (AA, ACOA, CODA, etc.), each set up to instruct participants in how to regain their sanity and stop rescuing.

(You again: "Gee, Merrill really *is* grumpy today. I'll bet she isn't getting enough vitamin B complex. Someone should check.")

If the characters in *Pretty Woman* had lived real people's lives, here is how the story would have continued after the movie. Longing to feel more legitimate, the Julia Roberts character would succeed in getting the Richard Gere character to marry her. And, feeling more legitimized, she would begin to build a sense of identity, power and self-worth, all of which would become threatening to the Richard Gere character even though she would be imagining that it made her more appealing. After all, the only reason she never moved in this direction before was her unfortunate social circumstances. Of course, she also loses interest in being at his beck and call, which is maybe when she notices that he has begun to withdraw emotionally. But who can blame him? He feels hurt and betrayed. This is not the woman he married. And so he secretly starts searching for another naive, joie-de-vivre-driven, beck-and-call girl to serve his needs. In other words, if I am not mistaken, *Pretty Woman* turns into the story of Donald and Ivana Trump and Marla Maples!

Well! Now that I have proven how pernicious this whole

rescuing business can be (in fact, it's even at the core of that most pathetic of female situations—waiting for the unhappily trapped married man), then what, oh what, you are probably wondering, are we to put in its place? How do we rebuild our romantic fantasies? Well, I think there is a solution. And, as they say on the sitcoms, "It's kinda crazy but it just might work."

Here it is: Entertain the notion that the rescuing isn't what we crave. After all, there's a lot of *work*. Couldn't it be the theatrical behavior? All of those appealing facial expressions and great moves are being totally wasted on the wrong bunch of guys. And so I call for a national retraining program in which pleasant, good-natured accountants and management trainees can learn to pout and brood and wear leather jackets. One class could be devoted to the dramatic uses of staring into nature—the pounding surf, the driving rain, the howling wind. Learn which seasonal precipitate is right for you.

In other words, if we could just get the good, well-intentioned but dowdy guys to take all this over, it would be a whole lot easier and more doable than trying to get women like me to stop falling in love with the screwed-up, weaselly guys who use that behavior to such good effect.

Well, it's just an idea. I'm off now to see about some kind of meditation plan and maybe consult with a dietician.

Ah, Malibu!

Late the other night I was wandering around midtown Manhattan with a friend and we decided to stop into a pizza place on our way home. Not two minutes after we sat down, a big, drunk, insane guy reeled over to our table and stood teetering above us, with a hostile but fairly focused leer on his face. Then he picked our pizza up off the table, folded it in half and stuffed as much of it as he could into his mouth. "What do you think of that?" he asked us. "Very nice," I may have said, as I dragged my friend out of the building. When I looked back, I could see this human gargoyle wielding our pizza in his hands and lurching around the rapidly emptying pizza place. And I thought to myself, Boy! Is it any wonder that everyone loves New York City! Where but here would a perfect stranger care enough to come into my life for the express purpose of keeping me from needlessly consuming several thousand empty calories at the very time of night when they would certainly do the most damage!

Yes, New Yorkers are a special lot, all too aware of how much they've been blessed. But now that I am spending time in the West, I feel I must share some of the glories of the community I call my home. I'm speaking of Malibu, California—fabled in story and song. Here are some of its many real advantages.

Life in Malibu Is Worry-Free.

Why? No daily experiences! At least not of the type you might face if you lived in a real city. Say good-bye to stimulus overload. There's only one movie theater, and it's always showing something you want to avoid. Plus, it's about an hour's drive to anything except the beach, which gives you all the time you'll ever need to become obsessed with yourself. Jog! Surf! Hire a trainer! Have a colonic! Watch your skin grow leathery in the sun! This kind of life will not only provide you with an automatic peer group but will tone you up, give you a warm, healthy glow and turn you into someone who sidles up to strangers and says, "Hey! Punch me in the stomach! It won't even hurt me. Go on. I dare you. Punch me in the stomach!"

You may never hear another depressing conversation. Residents of a major metropolitan area like New York overhear many odd bits of talk in the course of a day and often find themselves accidental participants in the morose or peculiar ramblings of people they would rather not know. This can happen on subways or ferries, in buses or taxis, in elevators or in the crowded streets. But it can never happen in Malibu because we do not have any of these things to speak of. Not even the streets. Oh sure, you may occasionally come into contact with residents while waiting in line at the market. Or during the summer if you go to the beach. But even on the chance that you happen to overhear them talking, you will find that surfing and hair care are their preferred topics. These are by and large simple, happy people for whom the word *umm* has a thousand and one meanings. "Umm, what?" they might say, for example.

After your arrival, you'll notice there really are a lot more fit-looking people per square inch. There's a very good reason for this:

There Are No Good Restaurants in Malibu.

Okay, there is *one* pretty good one. But you know you're in dining hell when you can recite the daily specials out loud right along with your waiter. The attitude of the other eating places for miles around is "We don't *have* to be any good. After all, we're right by the beach." Consequently, most of them offer the unbeatable combination of mediocre food and exorbitant prices. Add to that the slow but casual service of stupefied waiters and waitresses and you have Malibu dining at its finest. "I don't *have* to be here," even the busboy seems to be restraining himself from telling you. "My father owns Twentieth Century Fox except okay, like he *made* me get a job this summer but he can't make me act like I *like* it."

Not every restaurant in Malibu is right on the beach, but

even the ones without proximity are kind of suspect. The best sushi bar is right next to a bait shop, and the main seafood supplier shares a building with a plumbing concern. All these elements combine to create what I like to think of as a quick, effective and permanent weight-loss program for the residents. But this is not the only personal-appearance advantage of the area.

It Is Easy to Be Stylish on a Low Budget in Malibu. Why? Because the opportunities for convenient shopping are almost nonexistent. The central shopping area consists of a few gourmet-cookware stores, some novelty gift boutiques and a couple of clothing places featuring outfits so trendy that you may find yourself embarrassingly out of style by the end of the day. Which is actually not even a problem as long as you stay inside the city limits, where it is almost impossible to look out of place based on dress code. This is one of the things I like most about Malibu. When I lived in Connecticut I frequently got the impression that my informal clothing offended long-standing community sensibilities. But in Malibu I could show up for dinner dressed in a mattress cover, a porkpie hat and wing tips and no one would insist on seating me back by the men's room.

Of course, there are drawbacks to living anywhere, and I should point out that Malibu has its own anxiety-producing situations.

AH, MALIBU!

Malibu Anxiety.

Just as the New Yorker must always be ready for the mixed emotions that arise in an encounter with a disturbed person, so too must the Malibu resident learn to handle with unearthly calm the possibility of winding up in a checkout line behind Charles Bronson, Mick Fleetwood or Pia Zadora. Etiquette dictates that such situations be met with no facial movement. During one particularly trying week I not only ate dinner an arm's length from Ryan and Farrah but also saw Bob Dylan shopping for novelty items. As you can imagine, I was badly shaken by the whole thing.

Celebrity-coping is not the only stressful thing about life here. While exhibitionists are an unpleasant fact of life in New York, anyone who has seen nude bathing in my neighborhood knows *that* is no piece of cake either. You are in constant danger of running into not just your neighbors but your trusted public servants covered with sand and flapping about in the raw. Do you really want to see your mailman with his clothes off? I know I didn't.

And I haven't even touched upon the bench in the center of town that commands, LOOK. SEE. FEEL. BE. LOVE. After a challenge like that, you will find yourself feeling inadequate and probably in need of a nap.

And then there's all that commuting. Any job you take requires at least an hour of driving each way. Which causes a person to listen to far more talk radio than is good for mental health. The wide variety of radio shrink shows that is offered day and night in Los Angeles makes the Malibu resident susceptible to life questions such as "If I'm not the right person for myself, how will I know when I meet a person who's right for me?" Which brings me to my biggest complaint about the area:

There's Nothing to Complain About.

It's so pleasant and pretty, you really must find other targets for your whining. And those of us who count on whining as a form of relaxation have to import houseguests from out of town or take unpleasant lovers. Or write pieces intended to discourage any more people from moving out here. Remember, we don't have to be good. We're right by the beach.

THE WACKY WORLD OF MEN

So. The Men's Movement. What do we all think? Me . . . I can't take these guys seriously yet. I heard a guy whining about how there are no Men's Book sections at bookstores, and all I could think was, "Gee! and why are there no support groups for people in glowing good health?" Maybe what's needed are support groups for people like me, who have trouble feeling sorry for the people who already have the power.

I've been keeping an eye on the Men's Movement since the late Eighties, when I began seeing notices for "Men's Meetings" in alternative newspapers like the *L. A. Weekly*. It sounded so wacky to me that I actually attended the Tenth Annual California Men's Gathering. The theme that year was "Celebrate Men's Magic." "We want to celebrate the men who are vessels of courage, kindness, direction and magic in the world," said the brochure. So I went to get a firsthand look at a few of these vessels.

It was a three-hour drive up to a retreat at Big Bear Lake, in the San Bernardino Mountains. I remember making a left turn at the concrete deer, and then driving many miles down a winding dirt road until I became concerned that I had gotten the directions all screwed up. That's when I noticed, before me, a group of oddly dressed men free-form dancing in a big open meadow.

I sensed immediately that this might be some of that men's magic I'd heard so much about. Especially after I noticed the guy with the white ponytail did not appear to be wearing any pants. He was arm in arm with a man dressed in a red kimono and a baseball cap. As they turned, I was able to see that the nude guy was in fact wearing a G-string . . . a detail that, quite frankly, did not much improve the overall look of his ensemble. But I had been warned. The orientation booklet with which I was provided had said "You may find that some of the people here dress or behave in ways that make you feel uncomfortable. You may be uncomfortable with a man wearing a dress. You may wonder who is gay and who is straight and who is bisexual. So do we."

Since feeling uncomfortable around men is a specialty of mine, I knew I was in the right place. A bearded fellow in his thirties who introduced himself to me as one of the organizers of the event as well as one of the editors of something called *The Men's News* explained to me some of the reasons he thought men might want to attend a gathering of this type. "Because the role models we grew up with aren't functional anymore," he said. "Men are barraged with

'It's *your* world and *you* fucked it up.' Even men in power are very hurt men. Most men get a lot of hurts and it's not okay to talk about them."

And so, toward that end, the presumably hurt men attending the Tenth Annual California Men's Gathering were offered communal dining, campfires, seminars and workshops with titles like Male Strength/Male Truth or Men Nurturing Men ("This workshop will involve rapping, nurturing and stretching boundaries."). Or The Joy of Men's Liberation. "The focus of this workshop," said the black-and-yellow orientation book (whose cover was emblazoned with a graffiti-like symbol of a dancing man), "will be for each of us to clarify the truth about our wonderfulness as men." The orientation book was awash in this kind of language. Consider, for example, the Guidelines for Twinkling: "Sometimes in a group discussion you may want to agree with what someone is saying," it read. "If your feelings resonate with their comments yet you have no need to add to them, you can express your support by twinkling. Raise both hands, palms forward, and wiggle your extended fingers." Now, I personally have never met a man who would voluntarily (or even under duress) participate in *anything* called twinkling—not even a violent sport in which people got punched and cars exploded. But then, to be fair, I never saw any twinkling taking place during my day at the Men's Gathering. I did, however, hear someone call out, "Bravo!" during the "Love and the Nature of Relationship" seminar, where a man got up to share his idea of "Having an affair with myself." "I have to be Mr. Right for *me* before I can be Mr. Right for someone else," he said. This was not the only time that afternoon that it occurred to me that the budding men's movement seemed to have already been co-opted by the editors of *Cosmopolitan.*

I discussed the all-important question of image with a man who introduced himself to me as Sasha. He was a self-described "former Buddhist priest Jewish psychologist." "How this is going to look to mainstream America . . . *that's* what we have to craft," he said to me that day. "A lot of the men here are so idealistic that they want to do this spontaneously and I say to them, 'Guys! We have to craft this. We have to think marketing psychology and we've got to tailor this to the mainstream.' "

One subtle but important image change since that time seems to have been the addition of the Indian ritual "the sweat lodge" to the movement's male bonding activities. Back on that day in the Eighties, they had instead something they were calling the Pagan Empowerment Circle, described in the literature as "an event for all who want to see a healing male energy emerge on the planet." Previously it had been called the Faerie Circle, and the year I attended they were thinking of a return to that name for tradition's sake. But as far as "the mainstream" goes, it seems apparent that many more men would be willing to admit to having spent the weekend at a sweat lodge (or anything involving the word sweat) than at a faerie circle (or anything involving the word . . . well, you know).

I audited quite a few other workshops during my day at the Men's Gathering. I was asked to leave Friendship Between Males: An Art Therapy Workshop, in which several dozen men, seated at long worktables, were instructed to clip out magazine photos and make collages illustrating the questions "How do male friendships start? What brings you together with other men?" The orientation of the class was to be strictly male, I was told.

Hurt, but not very, I stopped by the room directly adjacent, where I was in for quite a surprise. The Creating Erotic Poetry and Prose workshop was being taught by Mr. Dances-with-a-Bare-Butt, the guy from the field. Fortunately, in his role as a teacher he had selected the pants option.

"He's a psychologist from the Valley," Sasha whispered to me. "He's also a performance artist and he has cross-dressing parties at his house." Mr. Butt-man introduced himself to the class as Howard and explained that our goal was to create a group-written poem about one of the men in our midst. I don't know if this is the kind of thing men would do more of if they weren't being held prisoner by their fascist image-keepers, but a long-haired blond guy in a red beret immediately volunteered himself as muse. "His ringlets cascade over his shoulders," an older man threw out as a first line for the poem. "Yes! Yes!" Howard encouraged him, "Someone write this down!" "His hair is golden in the afternoon light," said the next man as we went around the classroom adding lines. "His hands are folded in front of his genitals," said the next contributing poet as I suddenly began to get more vibes that told me it was time for me to go elsewhere. And a good call it was, too, because when I checked back less than an hour later to hear how the poem was turning out, Howard and two of his students were totally nude.

Meanwhile, in a workshop nearby, about thirty-five men with their arms outstretched were moving in circles on their tippy-toes as they took part in Movement for Men. "It's good to know where you are with yourself before you touch another person," I heard the instructor say as he began the next exercise. I never heard what it was supposed to accomplish, but by the time I decided to call it a day, it looked like a slow dance at the senior prom.

On my way out, I gathered up some of the free reading material—pamphlets and booklets that I have kept to this very day. One booklet called "Male Pride and Anti-Sexism" contained this advice in a list of "Individual Actions Men Can Take": "Buy yourself some flowers and let the florist know they are for you." There it was again! The voice of Helen Gurley Brown! How does *she* weasel into every sexual movement? But then I thought to myself, well, I guess turnabout is fair play. Why should men have gotten through the twentieth century untouched by this kind of goofy rhetoric? Women had to learn how to live with it and retain their dignity. However, I feel compelled to offer a warning. If the Men's Movement isn't careful, men's magazines full of articles titled "Finding the Haircut That's Right for Your Face" or "Ten Terrific Ways to Tighten Your Tummy" or quizzes about love compatibility can't be far behind.

Bob the Dog
(1974–1988)

About a month ago my older boy, Bob, started acting sick. He was fourteen (which, of course, is ninety-eight to you, me and Lorne Greene), but his problems weren't only about being an old guy. Suddenly he just wasn't what he used to be. At first this was kind of a blessing because what he used to be was a dog who would stop at *nothing* in his quest for things he felt might possibly turn out to be food.

Bob wasn't content to wait until that part of the day when the green plastic dish full of gelatinous glop would descend. On more than one occasion he actually stole and flattened several sealed cans of food from a not-quite-unpacked case in the kitchen. By the time I discovered the remains, he had extracted all the contents in such a way as to leave the empty containers looking like overworked summer-camp copper-tooling projects.

WHAT THE DOGS HAVE TAUGHT ME

For Bob, the word *edible* had the broadest definition. Where food was concerned, he was a freethinker. Earlier this year, for example, I came home to find that my art portfolio had been removed from where I had wedged it between a filing cabinet and a dresser. It had been opened carefully, and several of my graduate school watercolors, including my self-portrait (which took me quite a few weeks to paint), had been removed and partially consumed. For a brief moment I wondered if a uniquely frightening psychotic criminal had begun a fiendish campaign of terror against me. On the bright side, Bob was able to bring an interesting new visual metaphor to what had been kind of a traditional painting.

Looking back on his life, I would have to say that this was his most creative phase. It was during this period that he ate my Scrabble board, a lot of my dictionary and about a third of Joseph Heller's *Good as Gold*. (Perhaps he would have eaten more if he'd had a chance to eat *Catch-22* first.) In fact, Bob got so creative with eating that it was hard to guess what things to try to keep away from him. He ate a Prestolog. He opened a closet door and removed a sealed box from the second shelf, deciding for reasons of his own to eat my antique Christmas ornaments. In the process he also managed to get a decorative fishing lure lodged in his front paw, which meant that I had to get in the car and haul him into town to an emergency room at 2:00 A.M. to have this particular snack item surgically removed.

All this was tame compared with the time I found him relaxing in the backyard, gnawing on what looked like an amazingly lifelike cat hand puppet. I still don't know if the skunk met the same fate, but I do remember with clarity the end result. After we'd drenched Bob in many, many cans of tomato juice, which everyone said would neutralize the odor, he looked and smelled like an Italian *marinara* dish from hell. And of course he spent the rest of the day trying to drink his own back. These were truly the magical times—rationalizing the death of some small creature that never imagined itself as somebody's hors d'oeuvre. Bob's life was, on occasion, devoted to murder as well as mayhem and dinner.

Happily, he sometimes resorted to ingenuity rather than cold-blooded homicide. He even figured out how to open the refrigerator. One night we found him cheerfully seated in the corner opposite the fridge, doing the doggie equivalent of a smile and wave, several inches from an empty Styrofoam steak tray and a piece of plastic that had once held a giant block of cheddar cheese. Bob was calmly finishing off an apple core. Not far away was a plastic supermarket sack containing two untouched zucchinis. Apparently when he was constructing his dinner menu, he decided to forgo the vegetable dish.

Bob wasn't a great-looking dog, and for most of his life he had a weight problem. Vets listed his breed as "German shepherd mix," although it always seemed to me that he had less shepherd than German waiter or chef. Once when I went out to the store, he removed a pot of split-pea soup from the front burner of the stove, carried it into the living room and ate it without spilling a drop. If we lived in a more perfect world, he might have had the chance to make a very fine busboy for some restaurant. At least they never would've worried about scraping the dishes off before loading them into the dishwasher.

He did goofy things in his short life—such as jump at birds who were circling several hundred feet above him. But he wasn't a stupid dog, if you define dog intelligence as the ability to solve problems (and if you can define dog problems as worth solving at all). When he and I first started living together, I intended to keep him in the backyard—a situation he rectified the first day. By the time I got home from work he had removed the lower five panes of glass on a jalousie window and made himself a very handsome doggie door. That was the last time I bothered trying to lock him out. It was futile. He would eat through wood. He would break through glass or screen. No Cyclone fence could hold his big fat body. He was driven, ever driven, by the insatiable need to get from wherever he was to the other side of everything and anything. It cost me several thousand dollars in fence repairs when he escaped from the backyard to a place in the front yard where he sat patiently waiting to be let back into the house so he could eventually get into the backyard again. I like to think he appreciated the Zen truth of this.

And then there were the Manhattan days, beginning with that first early-morning walk down Sixth Avenue to the park when Bob came to a screeching halt to take a dump right in front of the Magic Pan. Dog ownership in the Big Apple is unlike dog ownership in any, less complicated, suburb. In the deepest, darkest part of the night I would awake to find him gently nuzzling my neck—a signal that in California would simply mean I had to open the back door but that in Manhattan meant that I had to get up and put on all my clothes, including shoes and socks (not to mention appropriate seasonal gear), and accompany him down to the street to deal with an emergency I dared not question but that sometimes turned out to be that he thought he had heard something.

On the plus side, being a dog owner in New York brought a new intimacy to the relationship between owner and dog, as I found myself relating to details of the dog's digestion in ways I'd never before dreamed of. I'm ashamed to admit it, but in California I never accompanied my dogs out after dinner (although I guess the opportunity was always mine for the taking), but once in New York I was able to see really close up just how well the dogs were enjoying—and digesting—their meals. There were other benefits too, such as interaction with the neighbors. It can be a real icebreaker when someone calls from two to twenty stories above, "Get your damn dog away from there!"

It was during our years in New York City that I came home one evening to find that Bob had eaten a jar of pills the vet had prescribed for my other dog, Stan. I never knew if the pressures of city life were responsible for this sudden drug problem, only that I had to pour hydrogen peroxide down his throat to induce vomiting and then follow him around for the rest of the evening, cleaning up after him. (I'm told this is also the procedure they used on Liz Taylor at the Betty Ford Center.)

It was in Manhattan that the dogs decided no apartment

was big enough for the two of them and set out methodically to reduce the indoor dog population to one. The hired dog-walker would call with the news that skirmishes had broken out and all parties were waiting for me at the hospital. It was amazing to think of Bob in a fight of any sort because, quite frankly, he wasn't much of an athlete. Stan always enjoyed a rousing game of fetch, but Bob preferred to play "I'll Just Get the Ball and Eat It."

Bob forced me to learn some hard lessons, such as: Bob should never be let off the leash. I learned that when I took him running with me in the park. It had seemed so idyllic— a girl and her dog. Until I turned back to check on him and discovered that he was nowhere to be seen. After three long hours wandering the environs, calling his name in increasingly panicky tones, I headed back to my car, some six blocks away. It was sunset, and I felt sure he was dead or gone. Until I actually got right up next to my Honda and, of course, there he was, sitting in the front seat, with a trail of doggie toenail marks all the way up the door to the window. I guess he'd just figured, Screw this exercise stuff! and decided to leave me to it.

Which reminds me of the other time he disappeared, before I installed the second layer of fence in the backyard. I live near a highway, and as the evening wore on and things were beginning to look grim, I got out the big guns. I stood out in the street and yelled, "Dinner! Bob! Dinner!" When he wasn't home by dawn, I was sure he was now just an area rug. But bright and early the next morning the neighbor who had accidentally trapped him in her backyard released him. I realized that he must have lived through a very peculiar kind of torture that night. There he was, only a few feet from me yelling "Dinner!" and probably thinking to himself, *Damn! I can't believe it. The one time that she has a second seating and I can't make it.*

Yes, we shared a lot of special moments, my dog Bob and I. Or at least I shared them. I was never sure if he was paying attention, which is similar to the problem I often have with men. But I cut Bob a lot more slack because he was a dog. I mean, after all those years he still didn't know what I did for a living. So it's a pretty fair tribute to his charisma as a dog that I miss him as much as I do. I miss him a lot. Though reading back over this piece, it's pretty hard to say why.

LIMO TO HELL

My recent invitation to the Emmy Awards got me thinking that the whole premise of the Emmy telecast is a little confusing: that each year there is so much incredible stuff on TV that it is not possible to contain the orgy of awards and self-congratulations, speeches and production numbers in a less-than-four-hour show.

I know this probably sounds jaded. I guess even *I* had some hopes of an evening of grandeur and glitz the very first time I attended. I fretted for weeks with all the women I knew on the topic of proper attire. I even purchased several outfits so unlike the kind of thing I ordinarily wear that I began to question everything that I knew to be true about the order of the universe.

When all of this dawned on me—the night before the event—I returned the beaded-and-sequined funeral wear and bought myself a woman's tuxedo. I think it was that same evening that my escort and I made the momentous decision to eschew the traditional complimentary limousine and drive ourselves to the big event in his car.

Now, I know that probably sounds goofy if you are one of those people who have always longed to ride in a limousine. But riding in a limousine makes me feel like a geek. First of all, there is the preposterous size of the car, and then there's the *Upstairs, Downstairs* effect concerning the amount of room *you* get versus the amount the driver gets. It's so unlike anything I was taught to be comfortable with that it triggers in me a compulsively compensatory behavior, and I end up encouraging each driver to pour his heart out to me in ways I would generally discourage, even among beloved family members.

And so, on previous limousine rides I have heard (at my own request) the sad tales of the overwork, poor pay and stress that sometimes constitute a limo driver's life. I have listened to stories of abuse suffered at the hands of callous celebrities (one driver told me Warren Beatty made him sit outside a restaurant for sixteen hours and, when he finally came out, didn't even tip him). And then there was the time I listened in polite horror to an excruciating description of the congenital defects of a driver's grandson. Also hard to forget is the time that I looked into the rearview mirror only to notice that my elderly, bloodshot-eyed driver was taking the limo to sleepyland. I was able to rouse him with a brisk slap on the cheek and talk him into making a pit stop at the nearest Denny's, where I watched him drink cup after cup of black coffee before I would agree to get back into the limousine.

LIMO TO HELL

Glamorous Emmy Story Number One

So, driving ourselves seemed like a fine idea to me, right up until the time we joined the unmoving crunch of grid-locked limousines that had converged on the Pasadena Civic Auditorium like salmon headed upstream to . . . well, I guess to attend some kind of big salmon media event. The increasing frustration of moving only a vehicle's length per green light was starting to make my sometimes fiery-tempered escort kind of fiery-tempered. Which is why, as soon as he had an opportunity to make any turn that led out of this morass, he did so, even though that meant we were traveling *away* from our destination.

This eventually led us to abandon our valet parking pass and park the car in a department store lot some six or eight blocks away. Next came a brisk walk through two very ex-pansive department stores, followed by a very unpleasant high-speed footrace down many long blocks of city streets in over-a-hundred-degree heat. My escort maintained a con-stant fifteen-foot distance in front of me, glancing back only occasionally and gesturing significantly at his watch. I hob-bled gloomily behind in a pair of high heels, growing in-creasingly damp in my wool-blend tuxedo and nylons. The good times continued after we were seated. From that mo-ment straight through the last song-and-dance extravaganza involving extras dressed up as cartoon characters, my escort subjected me to a continuous harangue as he grew more and more panicky about the safety of his car in a department-store lot. "You're sure you don't think they're going to lock up the place before we get out of here?" he kept asking. "You think it's okay, right?" About the thousandth time he asked, I turned and looked across the aisle. And there was Bruce (*Scarecrow and Mrs. King*) Boxleitner, knowing he looked cool as he ran his hand through his tousled sable hair.

Glamorous Emmy Story Number Two

Last year I decided to chuck the tuxedo effect and I went out and bought myself a swell new dress. No one was more amazed than I that I was able to find one I liked, could afford and in which I actually seemed to cut a dashing figure. To protect my new acquisition from the assorted ink and marinara and condiment stains that I manifest like an uncontrollable form of stigmata, I never even took my dress out of the garment bag in which it had been hermetically sealed at purchase.

Emmy day started smoothly. This year my escort was once again planning to drive himself, but *I* was sharing a limousine with a group of friends. Yep, I felt pretty good, right up until the first breath I exhaled as the limousine pulled out of my driveway. It was then that I learned that the belt to my dress, the centerpiece of the design, had been constructed by the Morton Thiokol company. It somehow lacked an adequately engineered system of fastenings—it merely had a thin and useless loop—and in fact slid right off my body every time I breathed out. Maybe this was my fault. Maybe there was an elaborate system of hoists and pulleys that I should have asked to be hooked up to at the store. But now there seemed to be nothing I could do. I experimented during the drive with doubling the belt back on itself

as well as with a form of breathing so shallow it probably
could not be sustained in cryogenic suspension. As I walked
up the auditorium steps I was so preoccupied by the issue
of how to carry my purse and my program *and* keep my belt
on my body that it took me a couple of minutes to realize
that I was walking directly behind Little Miss I'm-Not-
Having-Any-Trouble-Keeping-All-My-Clothing-Looking-
Perfect herself, Cybill Shepherd. A gigantic wad of pho-
tographers clustered around her like iron filings. "Cybill,
hey Cybill! Over here!" they were shouting, and at any
angle she knew exactly how to make that I'm-a-gorgeous-
former-model-and-I'm-not-having-any-belt-problems-at-all
face right to the camera.

My worst fear was naturally fated to come true: I actually
won something and had to make a long, graceless, belt-
clutching walk down the aisle to the stage, all the while
being scrutinized by a mobile hand-held camera. Of course,
it wasn't only me. . . . I was enveloped by a group of eleven
men with whom I shared the honor. I think I do have the
distinction, however, of being the only winner with just one
hand free with which to receive the award.

But the glamor didn't stop there. After the show a group
of us decided to get together for a celebratory dinner. My
escort, as mentioned earlier, had his car there and insisted
on driving part of the group. Which is why I found myself
sharing the crawl space behind the seats in a two-seat sports
car with another good-natured but secretly irritated woman
also dressed in formal wear and also being strangled by her
various matching accessories. When at one point along the

way the car screeched to a halt to obey a traffic light, I almost became the first person in history to meet her death by being impaled on an Emmy. Which brings us to this year.

Glamorous Emmy Story Number Three

This year my escort and I *both* took the limousine, which, of course, came with the usual drawbacks. Before we left the driveway I learned that our driver had been a cool-guy senior at the high school where my escort had been a dorky freshman. This poignant example of life's cruel ironies depressed me all the way to the gridlock. But we live and we learn. This year when my escort tried to talk me into another formal-attire footrace in the scorching heat, I was able to respond with a jaunty, heartfelt obscenity. And this year, although I chose for my outfit precisely the same thing as last year, my sturdy, unmatching belt stayed exactly where I put it. But even these impressive accomplishments were faint consolation for what turned out to be a night of pure, uninterrupted tedium. You must remember that when you attend a live television show, you do not have your usual remote control changer option.

My escort was called backstage early on, and I was left to spend the duration of the evening with a "seat filler." These are people hired by the networks to show up in their formal wear and occupy any seats abandoned by audience members who are losing their will to live. In this case, a *very* large, round, pale gentleman with a new growth of beard became my new companion for the evening. Which is only one of the reasons that hour three found me pacing with others in the lobby. By the time I rejoined my escort during hour four, we were both so shell-shocked by boredom that we elected to stand in the back of the auditorium. This afforded us a vantage point from which little could be seen, which in this case didn't turn out to be a drawback.

The following day I spoke to a friend who had attended with a guy who had never been there before. On the ride over, in the limousine they shared, this friend opened a bottle of champagne and proposed a toast: "To the most boring evening of your life." The first-time guy became enraged and lectured my friend about how jaded and cynical he had become. He made my friend feel kind of ashamed, until an hour into the show when they ran into each other in the lobby. "Let's get out of here," Mr. I'm-Not-Jaded said to my friend. "You were right." And they promptly took the limo home.

In the final analysis, it's very nice for anyone who works hard to receive an award for his or her efforts. But in the case of the Emmys, maybe it would be a good idea to try delivering the honors through the U.S. mail.

VIVA LAS
WINE GODDESSES!

So the other weekend I went to Las Vegas on a date. At first I had my doubts about our choice of venue, and consulted friends, who fell into two camps: those who found the excesses and depravities of the place to be the very definition of hilarity and those for whom the identical elements were at the heart of a searing existential depression, which, they felt, could only lead to a loss of the will to live.

I can confirm that there is real truth to both perceptions, and it seems to me that the best way to avoid passing from the first camp to the second is to be very careful about the length of your stay. *This must not,* for any sensitive and reasonably intelligent adult, *exceed thirty-six hours.* For those of us blessed (or cursed) with a hyperactive sense of the ironic, Las Vegas, taken in small doses, is a specialty act without peer. And so I present you now with a kind of handy guidebook for your own short visit. Think of it as something you might get from that *big* travel writer—I forget his name—the one who writes all the "Rome on five dollars a day" things, if he weren't too big a weenie to write it.

Merrill's Guide to Thirty-Six Hours of Vegas Fun

Las Vegas is but a hop, skip and a jump from Los Angeles. But since fewer and fewer people rely on any of the above for their transportational needs, you have your choice of flying or driving. We drove—through mile after mile of pale orange landscape, dotted with tiny specks of black and pale green that are either sagebrush or tumbleweed or rock—until we reached Las Vegas.

Of course everyone knows what the Las Vegas strip looks like from a million movies and videotape montages. But they ill prepare you for how really, really bizarre it is in three dimensions. Almost everywhere you look, a building is screaming a visual or verbal insanity at you. The overall effect is of something you made up in a feverish dream one night when you drank too much tequila and ate too many pepperoncini.

TIP NUMBER 1: STAY AT THE GAUDIEST HOTEL YOU CAN AFFORD. Why? Because the whole point of going to Las Vegas is to have the Las Vegasiest time you can have. I heartily recommend Caesars Palace, which I found to be the wackiest luxury hotel that I have ever been in, around or near. It's not just because the employees wear costumes or because of all the oversize antiquities, friezes and historical references. How about those moving sidewalks that carry you into the complex—passing through a miniature temple type of structure, with gold columns and horns to announce your arrival—and then abandon you to the regular old stationary sidewalks for your exit?

Many movies, such as *Rain Man*, have shown us in loving detail the lavish suites full of grand pianos and chandeliers that are provided for the high rollers. We, however, had an economy priced room right next to food services, just a short distance down the hall from accounting. This simple room did not have even a regular-size piano, but it did feature a giant raised marble bathtub. Okay, fine, I can definitely follow the concept of a giant raised marble bathtub/shower combo, but the concept kind of goes south in the small economy rooms where the tub has to serve instead of a stall shower. And since these tubs are located nearly in the center of the floor—only feet from the bed and the TV and the window—suddenly you are faced with a far-from-glamorous situation, namely, one where bathing must be done in the presence of all people in the room. This is less than ideal, *especially* if you happen to be sharing a hotel room with someone you barely know.

Now you might be muttering to yourself, "What kind of moron would share a hotel room with someone she barely knows?" but that is not something I want to discuss. This is, after all, my essay. The point I am making here is that maybe you never need to know someone so well that you lose altogether the option of showering privately. And in this particular room, your roommate, who may be pretending to sleep or watch TV, is, unquestionably, just watching you shower.

Which brings us to the in-house viewing selections. There

was a tape showcasing the various winning and dining opportunities in our very own hotel complex, such as "Cleopatra's Barge" for dancing and "The Bacchanal Room,"
where you dine in splendor, served by the lovely "wine
goddesses." There was also a learn-to-gamble-with-Larry-
Manetti tape that my date must have watched about 300
times. In this, a blond woman in a fur and the older guy
from *Magnum P. I.* who is not Tom Selleck take some point-
ers from Larry Manetti (I forget just who he is). But in a
hilarious twist of fate they end up beating him at his own
game . . . and then the fun begins!!!! Once your sides have
stopped aching from laughter (and once you have gotten over
the shock of showering in front of someone who doesn't mind
watching Larry Manetti for hours on end), it's high time to
get the hell out of the room and experience some of that
world-famous Las Vegas nightlife!

TIP NUMBER 2: GO TO A SHOW. Somewhere in your room
is a book that lists every show in town. I selected *Nudes on
Ice* for our viewing enjoyment because . . . well, it was the
stupidest-sounding show available. Now, I realize that not
everyone selects their entertainment according to this cri-
terion (and, by the way, aren't you glad you don't have to
travel with me?), but everything on the list sounded pretty
stupid to me, so I felt that attending the stupidest one of
them all would be the most Las Vegasy thing to do. (I actually
came very close to selecting *Boylesque*, but in the end I felt
that Las Vegas men pretending to be women would be less
interesting than the men pretending to be men and the
women pretending to be women.) And I was not disap-

pointed. I don't know whether or not partially nude women so bored with their jobs that they could barely keep their cigarette butts lit constitutes a "sexsational revue" (as the program advertised), but it was interesting to note that the more breast that was exposed, the less skating was required. I guess this equation is relevant in every walk of life.

Especially memorable for me was Act 5, which was called "A Russian Fantasy" and which seemed to my nonexpert eyes to be a re-creation of that period of Russian history when, because of a crop shortage or something, the czar apparently decreed that only a percentage of women in the royal court could be fully dressed.

Honorable mention goes to the comedian who came out and devoted a third of his act to dirty balloon animals (always a rollicking good time). This is entertainment that you cannot see anywhere else in the world, and for a very good reason. Why in the world would you want to?

TIP NUMBER 3: WIN A BUNCH OF MONEY. Let me begin this section by saying that I have never been remotely interested in gambling. I have always felt that nothing ventured is nothing lost. I have never been able to see the fun in losing $5 and then winning back $3.50. Which gives you an idea of the kind of stakes I usually play. But, influenced by my date, I picked the right number at roulette and immediately won $400. And before the evening was over, we had won $1,200. I cannot recommend this too highly. If it hasn't occurred to you, win $1,200 and see for yourself. It's very energizing and really adds to your Vegas fun.

TIP NUMBER 4: DINE AMONG THE WINE GODDESSES. By

now you will have seen the ad on your color TV (while you were trying not to watch someone else shower). What sort of Las Vegas visitor would you be if you didn't give the wine goddesses their due? At least this was my rap right up until we were seated at our table and I saw the wine goddesses in diaphanous harem outfits circling my date, offering to give him some kind of theoretical eye massage. Maybe I wouldn't have gotten quite so ticked off if there had been wine gods available for the gals. Maybe then we all could have had a great big laugh about it. Ha, ha, ha. As it was, I, for the first time in my life, felt it necessary to threaten restaurant help with my Swiss Army knife.

There were other highlights to the meal besides the much-loathed wine goddesses. For instance, it's not every restaurant that offers you what look like 3-D fiberglass replicas of the available entrées to examine before you order. For those of us who have never actually seen what a real veal chop looks like, this is extraordinarily helpful. But the biggest dinner highlight was definitely the arrival of Julius Caesar and Cleopatra, heralded by the crash of a giant gong. Dressed in full historical regalia, this important couple had come all the way through time with nothing more on their minds than to find out how we were enjoying our meal. And I confess I tried to use what little clout I had with the great Roman emperor to see about getting the wine goddesses pulled off the face of the earth.

TIP NUMBER 5: ON YOUR WAY OUT OF TOWN, BE SURE TO VISIT THE LIBERACE MUSEUM. Now, I don't want to say too much here. I know the man came to a tragic end. But let me just suggest that you slow down while passing through the portion of the museum devoted to Lee's brother George, and observe that in a glass case both his driver's license and his frequent flier card have been mounted and preserved. On sale in the gift shop are a variety of swell items. Because I was ahead my half of the $1,200, I was able to purchase the Liberace paper clips, the coffee mug, the photo-embossed Christmas ornament, the key chain, the extra-large postcard of Liberace posing by his closet and the box of scented soaps, each shaped like a grand piano and emblazoned with his name.

TIP NUMBER 6: NOW GET OUT OF THERE AND DON'T LOOK BACK. And so we say good-bye to the city of Las Vegas, remembering that we'd better not overstay our thirty-six hours. Taking with us a whole lot of free money and a bunch of silly stuff . . . and leaving behind the goddamn wine goddesses. And they'd better stay the hell out of Los Angeles if they know what's good for them.

AN INSIDER'S GUIDE
TO THE AMERICAN WOMAN

The first item in my collection of the greatest irritants of the early Nineties is the June 1990 issue of *Esquire* featuring "The Secret Life of the American Wife." On the cover is a partially clothed woman, anatomically labeled with such questions as "HER LIPS: Can you trust what they say?" and "HER BRA: What *really* keeps it up?"

I'm not surprised to learn that men are still mystified by women. Certainly women are still utterly baffled by men. But what I found so infuriating this time around was the type of thing the (presumably college-educated) editors and writers were pretending to find so gosh-darned unfathomable. And their approach! So *retro*, so Fifties, so "Honey, now dry those tears and how about we take you downtown and buy you something sparkly?"

The lead article ("Your Wife: An Owner's Manual") offered pseudoscientific dissections of such feminine mysteries as "HER HANDBAG: Its capacity and contents" and "HER PLUMBING: General Diagnostics." If this is how far men have come in their knowledge of women—to wide-eyed wonderment at the contents of her purse and dumbfounded speechlessness at the thought of "female plumbing"—well, I personally think now is as good a time as any to throw in the towel.

My suggestion to men is, *Stop trying* to comprehend that which is clearly too complicated for you. Let me kindly state that it no longer really matters whether or not you understand. I just don't think you should worry your pretty little heads about it for another moment. Instead, simply *memorize* the following information and blindly incorporate it into your thinking, much as one might deal with an elusive scientific concept, such as $E = mc^2$.

Merrill's Fun Facts to Know and Tell About Women

I. WOMEN AND THE ENGLISH LANGUAGE. To a woman, the words "I had a great time. I'll call you" translate roughly to mean, "He said he had a great time. He'll call me." So, if you *say* those words, expect to *make* a call to the woman to whom you have said them. If this does not fit into your plans, *do not say those words*. (I know this is confusing. Just memorize it and do it. There's nothing more to discuss.)

Women have other quirky language-oriented notions. For instance, to a woman the words "I love you" represent a heartfelt expression of the intensely fond feelings you have for her. At least, this kind of thing will be what the woman has in mind when *she* utters the words, and so she will not be pleased if your response is "Thank you" or "I know."

There is an interesting truth behind some of this that may be hard to grasp: Women *like* to talk about personal things. In fact, they actually *listen* when a man does just that. Why? Well, because women believe that a conversation can go beyond a simple exchange of sports scores! Yes! They do! In fact, women who meet for the first time on a checkout line will often have more intimate conversations with each other than they have had with men to whom they have been married for two or three decades. They do this voluntarily! Why? Because they find it *enjoyable!*

Now that you understand this, realize that the answer to "Hi, honey. What did you do today?" is *not* "I don't know. Nothing."

II. WOMEN AND FOOD. Most women are on a diet, thinking about going on a diet or wondering if they should think about going on a diet. In a free-market economy, a majority of women will order a salad on a majority of dining-out occasions. If a man wishes a woman to change her eating habits and make them more like his own, he need only repackage the food he would like to see eaten as a salad. For example, most women would feel okay about sitting down to a hot-fudge-sundae salad or a pizza salad.

It is not necessary to inquire whether a woman would like something for dessert. The answer is, *yes*, she *would* like something for dessert, but she would like *you* to order it so she can pick at it with her fork. She does not want you to call attention to this by saying, "If you wanted a dessert, why didn't you order one?" You must understand, she *has* the dessert she wants. The dessert she wants is contained *within* yours!

Bear in mind also that she wants you to keep pace with her and prefers you to eat at least half of your dessert because she does *not* want the responsibility of having eaten most of it.

III. THEIR ENTERTAINMENT NEEDS. Unlike men, most women are not endlessly in search of opportunities to watch things crash and blow up. Women tend to prefer movies teeming with human intrigue and personal foible to movies where someone breaks through a plate glass window with a car, or breaks a plate glass window with his fist, or breaks someone's head with his fist in a car, or breaks someone's fist with a plate glass window. We're just wacky that way.

IV. WOMEN'S ABLUTIONS (and why they take so long). The amount of time a woman takes to prepare for a date with a man is in direct proportion to the amount of time she has spent observing that man staring saucer-eyed at other women who have put in at least the aforementioned amount of preparation time on their date. If a man would like to see one decrease, so too must the other.

V. THEIR PLUMBING. How much should you know? Women are the ones who do not have a penis and did not even have to undergo painful penis-removal surgery to accomplish this. As a result, they will require more frequent stops on a long car trip.

Once a month women find themselves strangely depressed and taking a long hard look at where they've made a wrong turn in life. They will ruminate over such dilemmas as "Perhaps the reason I'm depressed is that I really need to find a better job, but I guess I'm afraid to change because I have such low self-esteem, which comes from my childhood when my mother always used to tell me blah blah blah blah blah." Then they realize they have just gotten their period, which snuck up on them in the form of a mood change. So if you get involved with a woman, don't be surprised when you find it sneaking up on you as well.

There are very simple ways to give a woman an orgasm. These involve specific manipulations of "the plumbing." If you suspect that you don't know what you're doing but think you are bluffing effectively and/or you notice that it is taking more than a half hour, please be advised that you're fooling *no one*. It's just that most women are too polite and too concerned about the frailties of the male ego to say anything. So ask the owner of "the plumbing" to provide you with some helpful tips!!! And save everyone involved a couple of long, painful hours!!! And by the way . . . if you *do* suspect that you don't know what you're doing, for God's sake, don't do it *harder*.

VI. Women and Love. I have heard men say that they don't mind the idea of breast implants in a woman because, after all, big breasts are big breasts. (Actually what I have heard men say is slightly coarser.) On the other hand, I have never met a woman who would rather be with a man in a toupee than a bald man.

This ability to accept and embrace the less-than-ideal, this generosity of spirit, has a downside—the tendency to be attracted to psychos. We know better, we're not proud of this, and we have spent decades learning that we would *really* rather be with nice men. But any man who has a problem attracting women because they think he is too nice would do well to augment his usual behavior with anguished exhalations of barely controlled rage.

In case you haven't noticed, women take sex just a tad more personally than do guys. For a woman, the only working definition of a one-night stand is a night spent with a guy who turned out to be a total weenie. The degree of any date's success can be easily determined by the degree of obsession it causes in the woman. If you would like to test this, introduce yourself to some of her good friends. If they aren't already sick of hearing your name, *the date didn't go that well*.

Once women are in love, they can be easily manipulated because they're so overwhelmed with feelings of insecurity. Many will happily take responsibility for everything that goes wrong, as in: "If he isn't happy it's my fault" and "If I'm not happy it's my fault."

Now that you know this, be a good guy and don't take unfair advantage. *Own up to stuff you know is your fault*. You might as well, anyway, because there is still another female phenomenon that ensures you'll be living on borrowed time if you don't.

VII. WOMEN AND THERAPY. Women are naturally attracted to therapy. Yes, it's true! If they don't get expensive one-on-one counseling, they will read self-help books and magazine articles or listen to radio and TV shows that discuss these issues or talk to and get advice from their friends who have done some or all of the above. Women do this because therapy actually involves so many of the things they enjoy: personal idiosyncrasy, a chance to talk dramatically about themselves and a good starting point for future conversations with friends or anyone they might meet in the checkout line.

VIII. Their Purses, Their Bras. A woman learns at a young age that she will be expected to carry the equivalent of a suitcase everywhere she goes for the rest of her life. And so she plans accordingly, secure in the knowledge that she will permanently have at her disposal anything, under a certain size, she might need in an emergency. This means that no matter what unexpected event or disaster she encounters, a woman will always have enough makeup to look really cute.

As far as the bra goes . . . give me a break, okay? *Give me a fucking break.*

My Career in Stun Guns

I live in Los Angeles because I am a frequent employee of what we refer to as the entertainment industry. And one of the by-products of that liaison is being "invited" to join an awful lot of labor unions. Which is why I've been a dues-paying member of the Writers Guild of America for about ten years, although I'd managed to avoid any gathering of more than three writers in one place at one time until last week, when I decided to go down to the Hollywood Palladium and see if I could find out why, as a member of the Writers Guild, I had been on strike for four months. This being my first-ever union meeting, I can offer no comparisons, except that I think there are probably fewer pudgy Minoxidil users in rimless glasses and sleeveless sweater vests in attendance at a giant meeting of the International Brotherhood of Teamsters.

As for the content of the meeting, it fluctuated wildly

between a very dull point-by-point reading of the proposed contract and some extremely raucous shouting, complete with the wild hissing, booing and cheering one might expect at one of General Noriega's rallies. There were no refreshments and no fabulous door prizes, and no one besides me was interested in doing "the wave."

Yet, while I had gone into the meeting unfocused, alienated and kind of irritated, I left feeling rather impressed by the passion that members seemed to have for continuing the strike. And in trying to cope with the idea of *even more* striking, I became aware that the reason I'd tended to avoid previous Writers Guild meetings was my growing disenchantment with the field of TV scriptwriting. So maybe my whole forced retirement was just a sign from God that it was time to select a more suitable career. Which is why I got up the next morning and started carefully reading the help-wanted ads, searching for beacons that might light the way to a brighter tomorrow.

I. Selling Stun Guns: A Career Just for Me?

No wonder I got excited. The ad said, "Make big money selling the revolutionary stun gun," and what little girl doesn't grow up hoping to hear herself one day speak the words "Any stun guns for you today, sir or ma'am?" Of course my heart was racing with anticipation as I dialed the number. A woman answered and told me someone would call me back. I didn't realize how unnerved I was by this until I heard myself tell her that my name was Monica. When the phone rang just a few minutes later, I jumped.

A man's voice said, "Hello, Monica?" and I felt the blood drain from my head. Just yesterday I had been a slightly respected member of the community, and now strange men were phoning me at home and calling me Monica. "What's all that clicking on the line?" the guy asked. "I don't like all that clicking. I better call you back." He hung up, and I briefly considered not answering when he called back. Maybe weapon sales wasn't the ideal career for me. "How about if I just come down to your headquarters?" is what I eventually said to the guy. "We don't have a headquarters," he told me, but he would "arrange to meet anywhere you'd like. We're a fly-by-night organization." "So I guess that means you don't have a medical or dental plan" is what I said, but I was thinking, *Boy! This is too good to be true! An opportunity to go to an undisclosed location and meet a strange man who is driving around with a trunk full of weapons! Pinch me! I must be dreaming!* "I'm going to have to think about it" is what I eventually replied as I reopened the want ads.

II. Stun Guns Part Two: The Adventure Continues

"Sell Stun Guns! Promote Peace! Prevent Violence! Make Quick Cash Daily!" said the ad right under the first ad. Now *here* was an attractive package—international diplomacy and high-stakes capitalism neatly rolled into one. Okay, I'd been burned before, but by now I kind of liked the idea of telling people that I was professionally "into stun guns." It had a crisp, dignified ring to it. So I dialed this number with a lot more enthusiasm and confidence—or at least that's what I thought I was doing until I heard myself tell the salesman who answered the phone that my name was Monica. "You have a nice voice, Monica," the guy on the phone said. "I'll bet you could sell stun guns." Suddenly I felt the room spinning and my skin growing damp and clammy— the combination of a goofy alias and a violent weapon being used in the same sentence was making me swoon. But on the bright side, this guy *did* have a headquarters, and so I found myself walking up to the door of a small white stuccoed house on a busy street, across from a retirement home and directly next door to COMPLETE BRIDAL SERVICE, EVERYTHING FOR THE WEDDING (which I figured probably was a prime location for this kind of business, considering the potential for shared referrals).

Outside the front door was a large, colorful lottery wheel, and beneath it was a crude painting of a rainbow with a pot of gold at the end. A man of about forty-five, sporting the always-fashionable Harpo Marx hairstyle, opened the door and invited me into a small but tidy living room. "Why are you looking around all nervous?" he said. "We're a licensed lottery dealer. That ought to make you feel safer." And of course once I realized that, I relaxed immediately—cushioned by the knowledge that lottery dealers are the moral backbone of every community. "Have you ever seen a stun gun?" he asked, instructing me to sit down on a sad old couch directly across from a large pyramid-style display of various hair-care products: shampoo, creme rinse, styling gel, mousse, extra-body conditioner . . . a perfect addition to the decor of any smart room.

My Career in Stun Guns

"Do you know what a stun gun is?" he asked, disappearing into a back room. "No," I loudly confessed, "I barely know what a creme rinse is." He returned and sat down uncomfortably close to me on the couch, removing from a box another black box about the size of a cassette player. "*This* is a stun gun," he told me. "When you push the trigger here, it sends out a jolt of electricity. It's 45,000 volts. It's the only legal self-defense weapon that you can carry concealed." He held the thing out in front of my face and squeezed the trigger, causing a bright blue miniature lightning bolt to jump from one point to another and causing me to jump from one point to another as well. "The way it works is we sell them to you by the dozen for $30 apiece, and then you resell them for $79.95 . . . but to tell you the truth, your personality . . . the way you react to the guns . . ." he said, hesitating, "well, it's obvious you're uncomfortable with them, and if *you* don't like them you're not going to have a lot of luck selling them." Somehow I knew there was a grain of truth in this. So I knocked him down and, grabbing the stun gun, zapped him. Then, when he was out for the count, I shampooed and moussed up his hair. (Okay, I made that last part up, but, as may be clear by now, I left there still thinking like a writer. I knew I hadn't found my new career yet.)

III. Ad Number Three:
My Career as a Professional Hypnotist

"Earn while you learn," the ad said. "No college education required." And while it was too late to do anything about erasing the latter, the idea of having my own little club act where I could wear a gown and humiliate audience volunteers had me nearly paralyzed with joy. Which is why I found myself in a room full of Naugahyde chairs in a building just a few doors down from the Hot Legs Boutique in midtown Van Nuys. We were a small group and so ill at ease that none of us could even look at one another, so we were relieved when a thirtyish man with a mustache (who looked like the "after" photo in a men's styling salon) came in and dimmed the lights. He instructed us to watch the TV monitor at the front of the room.

"We are gong to learn all about Marlo Thomas's unusual new movie with Kris Kristofferson," an announcer's voice boomed as we watched the opening credits for *PM Magazine*. "Plus, we'll find out about a *miraculous cure for everything!*" Right away I suspected that *one* of these two probably had something to do with hypnosis. And sure enough, seconds later we dropped Marlo like a hot potato and met Carol, a singer who was plagued by some kind of mysterious vocal obstruction until she turned to hypnosis, at which time, she said, she "discovered my own knowingness." Seconds later, Florence Henderson was seen chatting with Merv Griffin about how hypnosis allowed *her* to "go back in and clean out the areas of your life that bother you." (By this I assumed she meant that whole unfortunate Wessonality campaign, unless she meant those endless reruns of *The Brady Bunch*.)

When the segment was over, the guy from the styling salon photo rejoined our group. "What kind of people did you just see using hypnosis?" he asked us. "Were they reasonable people? Functional people? Normal people with normal problems?" No one said anything right away, maybe because we all had the feeling that the jury was still out on Florence Henderson. So to loosen us up a bit he had us go around the room and introduce ourselves. The girl with the fluffy hair was a receptionist at a local TV station. The white-haired guy next to her was unemployed. The hip-looking guy next to him was in music publishing and used to manage big money-making bands in the Sixties. And the oily-haired guy soaking in cheap cologne to my left was a security guard. As for me, I was just a happy little woman named Monica who had a dream of a nightclub career where I could take audience volunteers and stretch them out stiff as a board between two chairs.

With some annoyance the instructor informed me that this was not *that* kind of hypnosis. This was for midcareer people who want to work in a "therapy-related field" but don't want to spend eight to ten years getting a psychology credential. The twenty-four-hour beginning class ($295) would enable students to begin to see clients professionally *in just twelve weeks*. And by the end of the first year's internship here a trainee hypnotist could figure on making $20,000 to $50,000. As I looked over the application forms, I had to admit I felt spooked by the notion that in less than three months some civilian who wanted to stop smoking or who was experiencing stress might find him- or herself growing sleepy by gazing into the eyes of a security guard. Not to mention a guy who used to manage rock bands (although that certainly might bode well for the older groups in terms of future ticket sales).

"Anyone can print up a sign and just *say* they're a hypnotist," said our instructor, "but *we* are approved by the State Superintendent of Public Instruction." I thought about that and, deciding that the first way was more to my liking, headed out the door to check out the cost of printing up a sign. I had mixed feelings—sadness, because I hadn't found my new career, and happiness, because the strike had given me the free time to check out some very important new options. "Train to be a model, or just look like one" said the next ad on the page. Now *here* was a career that just maybe I could be comfortable with. I wonder what they pay you to just look like a model?

SHOWERING WITH YOUR DOG

I don't allow just anyone with mud on his tongue to fall asleep on me. (Well, not anymore. Not since the Sixties.) After several years of expensive therapy I've learned I have the right to require more from a relationship with a man. But, I must confess, it is the mark of how completely in love I am with my dog, Stan, that I almost always find this kind of behavior endearing in him.

Stan's status in my household has been steadily on the rise ever since that black day in September when the indoor dog population of my home was reduced by 50 percent. That was when half of my two head of dog went off to the giant overturned garbage can in the sky. At first I was concerned that the remaining member of the team would be lonely, troubled, maybe wracked with guilt, the way Timothy Hutton's surviving-brother character was in *Ordinary People*.

Then I began to observe that Stan was actually kind of glad Bob was gone.

I shouldn't have been too surprised. After all, on frighteningly frequent occasions over the years, Stan had, in a pretty straightforward fashion, tried to kill Bob. I always wrote off these murder attempts as poor impulse control rather than genuine malice-aforethought, homicidal-type acts. But now that it's completely apparent how much he enjoys the perks that come with being a solo dog act, I'm not so sure, especially after witnessing him nearly kill the puppy I briefly tried to add to our strange little family. And the fact is, he really *does* get perks now. For instance, I used to find it much easier to get into my car dogless when there were *two* dogs standing at the front door making those "we'd rather be dead than be left here" faces. I would think to myself, *Ah, screw it. They'll be fine. They'll entertain each other*. Then I'd leave the house with a clear conscience, imagining some kind of secret doggy confabs that came alive only in my absence—maybe intense, animated discussions of heartworms or something.

But when Stan stands *alone* at the front door making that "how can you do this to me?" face, I almost never drive off dog-free. My anthropomorphic fantasies rage much more violently out of control now that there's just one dog. Even at the expense of the reasonable maintenance of my car, which at this point is evenly coated with dog hair from stem to stern (including under the hood and inside all of the spark plugs).

On the plus side, riding around with Stan can be fun. It's

certainly much less stressful than riding around with the average man. For example, he always lets me pick the radio stations, and he greets my every choice of destination with boundless enthusiasm. And there are those special times when he leans over to nuzzle me with his snout—which I always take to be an incredibly moving tribute to the amazing bond that our species are able to share . . . until I remember, too late, that most of the times he does this he is simply looking for a cozy place to throw up. The most memorable instance of this was the time I was having the house fumigated for fleas and had been instructed not to go back inside for four hours. And so I was left trying to figure out an afternoon of activities appropriate for a woman covered with dog vomit.

I guess the point I'm getting to is that I'm completely off the deep end as a dog parent now that there is just the one dog, because in a lot of ways he seems like more of a roommate. And as a roommate, I have to say he's doing a nice job. Anything I prepare for dinner seems perfect to him. From a handful of popcorn to fettucine Alfredo to small, hard bits of gristle in a plate of warm beer (a personal specialty), he has never failed to exhibit anything less than exuberant delight in my menu planning. No man was ever this easy to please, that's for sure.

Okay, yes, there is a certain amount of unsavory cleaning to do out in the backyard, but it's actually minor compared to what's required after a man has blasted through a house like a raging tornado. And, yes, he does leave a lot of hair and stuff on the bed, but he also never hogs the remote control changer and forces me to watch hours of TV shows in five-second increments.

Unfortunately, there's a complication. Since I have conferred on Stan the status of roommate it has become increasingly difficult to compel him to undergo traditional dog humiliations. Like bathing. I used to tie the boy up in the yard and hose him down (the way you might, say, your parents) but that no longer seems fair. No basic pet-care book deals with this type of readjustment. And since it is my goal here to fill the holes that others never knew existed, I would like to help bring pet care into the Nineties, advising those for whom a pet is a significant other. Or if not, certainly an insignificant one. My first topic: showering with your dog.

Let's face it. Even the most beloved dog can be very stinky at times. And where pet hygiene is concerned, the enlightened pet guardian (and, of course, by that I mean me) has no choice but to share the indoor facilities with the animal.

Step 1: Choosing the Proper Wardrobe.

When showering with your dog, it *is* advisable to wear swim wear. I don't know whether the dog would know if you were naked, but *you* would know.

Step 2: Getting the Dog into the Shower.

Nothing can really proceed until this is accomplished. Often the dog will exhibit a little initial reluctance . . . perhaps because he has watched too many horror movies on TV in which showers are presented in an unfortunate light. Many dogs have never given any thought to the concept of "fiction" and so do not know that most showers are not just another death trap. Rather than confront the animal with a lot of mind-blowing philosophical concepts, I recommend one of two less complicated strategies that work for me. The first is what I call the old "ball in the shower" approach, in which you, the parent or guardian, relocate to the inside of the shower with some favorite sports equipment, making it appear that you have selected the location *not* because of its showering capabilities but simply because it is the best damn place for miles around to hit fungoes. If, after fifteen or twenty minutes of enthusiastic solo sports maneuvers, you have not managed to interest the animal in joining you, I suggest you switch to the immediately effective "chicken skin around the drain" approach. It's a well-documented fact that only a minute amount of chicken skin can accumulate in the lower third of any area of the world before it will be joined by a dog.

Once this has happened, simply close the shower door behind him, or pull the curtain. (For the more squeamish among you who worry about the mess in the shower, you can count on the dog to clean it all up. If he should happen to miss a little, and some chicken skin remains, don't worry. It will simply be taken by any future showerers as a remarkable indication of how seriously you scrub yourself when you wash.)

Step 3: Moistening and Soaping the Animal.

This may be trickier than it appears, because the animal tends to move to the parts of the shower where there is no water. And so it becomes your perpetual task to keep moving the water to the parts of the shower where there is a dog. During this phase, apply shampoo and try not to take personally the animal's expression, which indicates a hatred and loathing so extreme that he is trying to figure out how he can reconnect with his long-buried primitive instincts to kill and eat a human being. It may be useful to let the dog know that showering is not a punishment but something *you* actually find pleasurable and relaxing. If this does not help, now is an excellent time to explain to the animal that the legal system is built primarily around the rights of humans, and, if you want to, you can take him back to the pound where you got him and then his life won't be worth a plug nickel.

Step 4: Rinsing.

You are now dealing with increasing desperation on the part of the dog, who may be getting ready to make a break for it. This is why nature gave the dog a tail, to help you as you try to restrain him before he runs through the house all matted and soapy and gets big hair-encrusted stains all over your cherished possessions.

Step 5: Toweling the Dog.

This process is designed to help you avoid the splattered, soaking mess that results when the dog shakes himself off. No matter how diligently you perform toweling, it is futile. When you're through, the dog will disperse the same astonishing amounts of water and hair as if he had never been toweled at all.

SHOWERING WITH YOUR DOG

Now you may release the animal, perhaps deluding yourself that he is thrilled at his cleaner condition. You should
return immediately to the shower and shovel out the three
to five pounds of hair you will find lodged in your drain.
This brings me to the final but most important step.

Step 6: Remove Any Bottles of
Flea and Tick Shampoo.

Take it from someone who has lived through every unfortunate scenario that can result from simply leaving the bottle
around. . . . I know I have helped you.

MARKOE VS. THE STARS

Once when I was waiting around with much too much free time on my hands I started compulsively reading horoscopes in every magazine and daily paper I could find—hoping, I guess, to run into some specific good news that would herald the end to all my waiting. It was then that I began clipping them for comparison and to see which were coming the closest. I even sent away for a personal chart and a list of my particular planetary transits and daily predictions. Then I became aware of inconsistencies that were pretty hard to overlook.

My personal astrological profile, detailing where all the planets were at the moment of my birth and explaining what each position means in terms of my personality, says, for example, that my Mars in the eleventh house means I "enjoy athletic contests and competitions with friends." Well, *enjoy* seems strong, although it is true that I fake enthusiasm at baseball games in order not to seem like a drip. But unless drinking in restaurants can be considered an athletic contest or competition, I'd say the whole thing seems pretty far off the mark. Then there's Venus in Cancer (which means "involvements with deep emotional ties, faithful") versus Venus conjunct Uranus ("unable to honor deep commitments"). Or how about Saturn conjunct Midheaven, which indicates that I am "systematic, disciplined and orderly," versus Mercury trine Jupiter, which accuses me of being "sloppy, tactless, clumsy and lacking in self-discipline." I began to realize that all these contradictory, irresponsible characterizations about my life, all these false anxieties and false hopes, were providing the groundwork for a new kind of lawsuit. And so I present some of the evidence and exhibits I will be using when I haul the horoscope writers from all of the women's magazines, the *Los Angeles Times* and the *Los Angeles Herald Examiner* into court on charges of libel and breach of promise in the soon-to-be-legendary case of *Markoe* vs. *The Stars*.

Exhibit A: the alleged "fun day." Your Honor, a brief perusal of the events of October 1, 1987, will reveal that although it was predicted to be "a fun day when you feel satisfied and outgoing; entertaining, shopping for luxury and beauty items are favored," it was, in fact, the day of the big L.A. earthquake. Waking up to the house shaking and a TV screen full of panicky newscasters hiding under their sets could hardly be construed as "fun," and if anything takes the air out of shopping for luxury items, it's something that registers over six on the Richter scale.

On October 9 and 10, when I was promised "exciting new social contacts," my brother came for a visit. And, Your

Honor, this was during the same period when *Elle* promised me "good offers" that never materialized. When October 26 and 27 rolled around, I was pretty excited because I was told "mental brilliance opens unexpected doors." It sounded so promising I fairly bounded out of bed, and yet looking through my diary the only event worthy of recording on the twenty-sixth involved picking the chocolate off a Häagen-Dazs bar only to lose the ice cream part to the mouth of an airborne dog. On the twenty-seventh things were so slow that I had eaten dinner by 7:00 P.M. and was in bed watching TV when a friend invited me out to a restaurant. I was so eager for activity that I got dressed and went out and *ate a second dinner*. Now if *that* is an example of mental brilliance opening unexpected doors, I'm eligible for a MacArthur "genius" grant.

But you see, Your Honor, there were *millions* of incidents like this, not to mention more impressive breaches of promises that caused me such severe emotional distress and mental anguish that I deserve to be paid off with large sums of money. For instance . . .

Exhibit B: the infamous popularity watch of October 28 and 29. This one was a heartbreaker. Imagine being told "you are more popular and display much charm and grace." I quote from the events of the twenty-eighth as recorded that day in my diary:

11:45 A.M. No signs of a popularity surge thus far, but it's still early in the day and they say a watched pot never boils. [I don't usually use clichés in my diary, but I was planning to read this one in court.]

5:00 P.M. Now I'm starting to get irritated. No lunch

invitations. No phone calls. A special trip into town just to test my special new powers was embarrassing, and, moreover, I'm thinking that not only am I not more popular, maybe I'm invisible. And the scary thing is how badly all this reflects on tomorrow . . . when I begin my four-day run of emotional harmony and strong sexual attractions.

Well, Your Honor, suffice it to say that it would be a waste of time to detail what *actually* happened during my promised four-day festival of sexuality. Life is too short, and no one has *that* kind of time.

Worst of all were the weeks around Christmas, when so many different astrologers warned me to watch out for fiery-tempered arguments and separations from loved ones that I was almost afraid to buy gifts.

At least three different publications alerted me to possible emotional blowups on the fifth of December, "when you and a close associate both say too much and feel the pieces cannot be retrieved" (*Vogue*). I found myself tiptoeing through a day when the only thing that happened was that my car died. I did have to call a towing service, but I got along pretty well with the guy who brought the jumper cables. Eventually *all* of Christmas vacation had gone by, unmarred by a single fight or separation from a loved one. Not to mention no accidents (and I was advised that I was accident-prone, which made me nervous enough to nearly have an accident).

And so, Your Honor, when you take into account a ruined holiday season (and maybe I shouldn't even mention December 14, when Sydney Omarr specifically stated I would "be invited to a gourmet dinner by an attractive individual" and I ate at home by myself with the dogs, who *are* attractive but there are *two* of them) and the fact that *Cosmo* told me that this coming year my home is destined to become "a wild mix of fur-patterned fabrics—leopard spots on the floor, tiger stripes on the furniture" (something that gives me the shivers just visualizing)—yep, I'm pretty sure that I am owed a lot of money for the mental anguish, the broken heart, the broken dreams. From now on, *Cosmo* lady, confine your tiger stripes and fur-patterned fabrics to your own home.

ME AND THE GIRLS

"*He never has just one girlfriend. He always* has four at a time," my friend Amy tells me. She is describing what went wrong with the guy she just broke up with. (We'll call him Mr. X.) "Around *them* he'd be all nice and cool," she explains, "and around *me* he'd whine and cry. He'd be nice one minute, and then all of a sudden he'd be *totally mean*." Boy, does *this* stuff sound familiar. These narcissistic Peter-Pan-syndrome-type guys have been driving all of my girlfriends nuts for the better part of the decade. Happily, things are working out better for Amy with the new guy she's been going with, making her one of the few friends I have for whom love is going smoothly. Sometimes I think younger women have it a little easier. Amy is eight.

I think I liked boys when I was in the third grade, but I don't seem to remember anyone "going with" anyone. Of course, social patterns like this change with the times, and I for one intend to change with them, which is why these days I prefer to talk out my problems with Amy and her older sister, River, instead of with their mom, with whom I *used* to have talks of this nature back when we were both in college. Quite frankly, she's been married for a long time now, and I don't even know if she can relate to problems like Amy's and River's and mine. These old married types can really lose touch, as opposed to a hip contemporary gal like me who's been out there in the *real* world coping with subdeb and preteen problems for nearly twenty years.

"So this guy was playing around behind your back?" I ask, having been there myself. "He'd try and kiss all the sixth-graders," Amy tells me, breaking into an impersonation of him running around, crazed, making fish faces and squealing, "Oh, kiss me! Kiss me!" "What did the sixth-graders think of this?" I ask, thinking it pretty brave behavior for a third-grade boy. "They thought he was cute," says River, a gorgeous blond sixth-grader and one of the targets of the ill-fated kiss-me attack. "He *is* cute," says Amy wistfully, "but he's still a nerd."

"Then why did you *go* with him?" I ask her, playing naive but knowing in my heart that since I have already heard the dreaded word *cute* I have my answer. "How did it all get started?" "Well, they call you and you say, 'Will you go with me?' " she explains matter-of-factly. "You mean *you* said it to *him?*" I ask, fairly impressed. *I'm* not that bold. "Well, so after you guys were going together, then would you kiss him?" I ask. "*Nooooo!!!*" Amy shrieks, quickly reduced to that emphatic hysterical giggle that is the emotional cornerstone of embarrassed girls of all ages. "You *never* let him kiss you the whole time you went together?" I ask wide-eyed, now both curious and kind of basking in my own sophistication, knowing that a lot of times when *I* go with a guy, I *will* let him kiss me occasionally. (And quite frankly, it's not *that* big a deal.)

"So what made you decide to end the whole thing?" I ask as both girls peer at me through paper-towel tubes. "Well, she saw him kissing other girls," River reminds me placidly. (Oh, yes. Of course. This is the dude with four girlfriends.) Playing devil's advocate, I remind them that *she* wasn't kissing him, so why was that such a conflict? (I am being a dork here, I realize. I know damn well what the problem was.) "When you're going together, you're not supposed to *like* other girls," River points out. Well, true, those are the rules, and I for one stand behind them. But since the whole ugly multiple-kissing incident is now just a bad memory and Amy is now comfortable in a long-term relationship, it was River's sad tale of heartbreak and woe that made the strongest impact on me as our discussion of love and loss continued.

"I went with him for a year," she says quietly about her ex, whom we'll call Mr. Y.

"One day he called me up with his friend and told me he liked me. And asked if I liked him." She grows pensive as those tension-filled early days flash before her eyes. "So, I decided I kind of liked him. Actually, I usually wouldn't talk to him on the phone." "Before or after you were going with him?" I ask. "After," she says with a laugh, "although I never talked to him before, either." "But what does it mean to go with him if you're never actually talking to him?" I ask. At first, this does sound pretty funny. But about ten seconds later I'm thinking that in fact this always seems to be the case.

"He wasn't nice to me and wouldn't talk to me at school or anything. I didn't even *like* him the whole time I was going with him," River explains. By now this is sounding like a miniature of every troubled relationship I've watched come apart over the last fifteen years. Considering how young this stuff starts, it's no surprise that all my older friends are so exhausted.

It's getting to be late afternoon, and as on so many other afternoons spent with my girlfriends we have frittered most of this one away whining about guys. I try to shift the topic to something else. (Like there *is* something else. Ha, ha.) "If you could be anybody at all, who would you be?" I ask them. "Arnold Schwarzenegger," says River, without having to give it a moment's thought. "That way you wouldn't have to have a bodyguard." "I *hate* Madonna," says Amy, in a 180-degree turn from last year's position. "*Everyone* hates her now," River concurs. "I didn't used to know what she meant when she was singing," Amy explains to me. "For instance, 'Like a Virgin.' Back when I was five or six years old, I didn't even know what that was."

"So the girls at your school are not exactly interested in sex," I say cautiously. "*Eeeeuuuu!!! No!!!*" both girls scream at me in a unison so perfect they could almost be backup for the Supremes. "Well, how old should you be before you have sex?" I ask them. I'm just curious now. (Maybe I've *had* sex, and maybe I haven't. None of your beeswax.) But I *have* seen enough of *Oprah* and *Geraldo* to believe that even kindergarten students attend drive-in movies together these days. "In your twenties *at least*," screams Amy, making me feel a little bit better. (Okay, I admit I'm in my twenties at least.)

Yeah, we have entirely too much in common, River and Amy and I. The three of us spend our lives in turmoil and debate over constant problems with itinerant boyfriends. Then, of course, there's the other big problem area: parents. "My mom can be dorky at times," Amy tells me. I know what she means, my mom can be dorky too. "She acts like a nerd," River says, "and she *embarrasses* us. Like if a new friend comes over." Now Amy gets up to more clearly depict this ordeal by doing a lot of heaving and jerking motions back and forth across the room, serving to reinforce for me what a wise decision I made when I decided which half of this family I would hang out with.

Pacing around the living room now, River turns off the TV and is suddenly captivated by the colors it makes when the picture dwindles into a dot. Amy joins her, and the two of them stand there, turning the TV on and off, watching the colors start and stop over and over. "Ooooh. Baaaad," they scream in unison; it sounds as though only one person is talking.

So I join them. I'm no fool. I'm not averse to having some fun. "Ooooh. Baaad," the three of us say together as we watch the dot go from blue to green to purple and then disappear. The TV goes on and off yet one more time. I think we'd still be standing there now if their dorky mom hadn't made us all come in for dinner.

WRITE LIKE A MAN

*One thing I have plenty of is crackpot the-*ories about the differences between men and women. (In fact, I was one of the first to point out that our sexual organs are almost *nothing* alike.) And I stumbled onto another one this week when I bought a couple of trashy celebrity autobiographies at my supermarket checkout counter.

The two I picked—*The Boz: Confessions of a Modern Anti-Hero*, by Brian Bosworth with Rick Reilly, and *McMAHON!: The Bare Truth About Chicago's Brashest Bear*, by Jim McMahon with Bob Verdi—belong to the cute-guys-in-sunglasses genre. For readers who know even less about the world of sports than I do (and I doubt that's possible), I will say that both these people are good-looking white male football players in their twenties. Both have cool-guy haircuts and very hip-looking matching shades. And on that particular day in the supermarket, the depth of my uninterest in

the game of football, multiplied by the height of my enthusiasm for cute guys in sunglasses, gave me the impetus to
shell out the necessary dollars to make these purchases.
Which is how it came to pass that I actually sat down and
read the books and then came up with my new theory.

My New Theory

The parading of infantile character flaws as though they were
badges of honor and distinction is a male trait.

Consider the following examples: In a chapter of *The Boz*
entitled "The World According to Me," we are introduced
to "two people—Brian and the Boz." One of those two tells
us that "to people under thirty, or people who still had an
open mind, the Boz became a symbol of a new kind of hero:
somebody who wasn't afraid to give the finger to The Way
Things Are Supposed to Be and, at the same time, could
still accomplish great things." Presumably it is the Boz who
made the decision to begin his autobiography with the following passage: "Miami. The Orange Bowl. New Year's
Night, 1986. And I'm standing on the field between plays,
peeling a huge chunk of skin out of my hand and grinning.
I'm not talking about a little skin. I'm talking about *layers*
of skin, a big gouge of skin the size of a big broken rubber
band. And it feels good. . . . In fact, it feels great. . . .
The more skin the better. Pain and blood let you know you're
playing serious football."

A short while later, someone—I guess it is Brian—
laments, "Somewhere people got this barbarian image of
me. . . . I've learned not to let it bother me, but it used

to." But as we read on, we come to realize that both Brian and the Boz have a lot more on their collective mind than football. "To me, girls are just a pain in the ass," says I'm-not-sure-which-one. "They call at all hours of the night. . . . They leave notes with dirty messages on them." He goes on to describe a very overt pass made by a female fan one night in a bar. "It made me sick," perhaps-it-is-Brian bemoans, "partly because she was ugly. No, she wasn't even ugly. She was past ugly onto *ooooogley*." A little later in the paragraph he treats us to a sort of Joycean stream of consciousness on various women. "Kathleen Turner is a fox," he tells us. "Cybill Shepherd is not beautiful. . . . Madonna I like because she does her own thing. She's nice looking and she's got a hard body. . . . But she's probably got the intellect of a coffee table." And it's clear by now that we should take him at his word, since he may be one of the few writers today who has had sufficient one-on-one conversations with coffee tables to make this comparison accurately.

Moving on to *McMAHON!* we immediately hear a similar tone of voice. "I do carry myself like a bit of a hot dog sometimes," Jim says. "I'm not afraid of giving lip to some guy twice my size. . . . I was born to be a hellion." He then launches into reminiscences of his golden childhood. "I particularly enjoyed throwing things at moving objects, especially if these objects were the heads of classmates I didn't care for. . . . I was also very hyperactive . . . bored. . . . That still holds today. In kindergarten I'd take tacks and stick them in the fat rear end of this Hawaiian kid, who never did make it through the Pledge of Allegiance without screaming. . . . Then, they'd call my mom and she'd come in. Then they'd call the Hawaiian kid's fat Hawaiian mother and they'd all ask for an apology. . . . I still haven't said I'm sorry. . . . That kind of thing helped me get through the day."

The Boz also recalls the days of his adolescence fondly. For instance, "that summer I worked at this fast-food hamburger place—you'd know the name. And I used to do some horrendous things to people's hamburgers, just to break up the boredom. If I didn't like the person much, I'd rub his hamburger patty along the floor with my shoe before I'd cook it. . . . I'm not sure what makes me love pissing people off so much but I always have."

I believe that this kind of swaggering talk could only be published under the names of attractive successful white men. The combination of arrogance without shame and insensitivity without humility or hindsight is the sole domain of attractive successful white men. To test my thesis, I went searching for an example of a woman who was analogous in any way. I bought and read the autobiographies of the most willfully self-promoting and egomaniacal female media figures. And, after working my way through the writings of Joan Collins, Suzanne Somers, Shelley Winters, Tina Turner and Pamela des Barres, I couldn't help noticing that most of them were confessions about failed romances, family tragedies or personal foibles. Most were written in a sort of self-mocking tone. Pamela des Barres was even loving in her descriptions of crude sexual liaisons with narcissistic drug addicts. Not one of these women seemed to revel in their inadequacies the way the cute guys in sunglasses do.

So, kicking off what could be a trend for the Nineties, I would like to inaugurate the era of swaggering female autobiographies with chapter 1 of my brand-new work in progress.

THE MERR:

Confessions of a Great Big Loudmouthed Rude Girl,
as told to Helen Rogan

"December 20, 1979. 8:00 P.M. I am at the bar in a hip Los Angeles eatery, dressed in one of my smart little sport coat and slacks ensembles. I have just agreed to join a very attractive young television producer at his table for a drink, and as I head across the room carrying a brandy Alexander I feel the soles of my shoes hit a wet spot on the floor and then I feel my feet fly out from underneath me as I go into a seamless skid that sends me sailing like a cartoon animal clear across the room in one long, smooth movement that ends when I land underneath the table of my date. I peer out from beneath the tablecloth at a room full of horrified people, and then I rise to my feet, claiming to have engineered the whole thing. Maybe they bought it. Maybe they didn't. I just don't care. Because I know that the more hideously inappropriate my behavior, the more personal embarrassment I cause myself, the better. That's when I know I am playing serious comedy.

"Perhaps it all goes back to that day in the sixth

grade when I was experimenting with a tube of cream depilatory and accidentally removed most of my right eyebrow. As a result, I was forced to retreat behind a Band-Aid accompanied by a lie that had to do with somehow being attacked by a bird. Maybe, that's when THE MERR was born—and since that time I make no excuses. If people don't like how I do things I might yell sarcastic remarks at them and then lock myself in my room and pout for hours. Because I'm THE MERR and I guess I'm just the sort of a free spirit who does what she wants when she wants.

"And if that means living with a constant barrage of people coming up to me and saying, 'Did you cut your hair yourself?' or, 'Do you know there's a price tag hanging from your collar?' well, so be it! I do things my own way.

"Sometimes I'll just walk into a restaurant and sit down at a table and when they bring me my food, if it isn't *just the way I like it*, I'll probably eat it anyway and not say a word because I figure it's still a lot better than anything I would have cooked for myself. And at times like these I might toss back my wild mane of raven hair and break into a gale of gleeful laughter. And in so doing maybe get a great big marinara stain all over an item of clothing that I paid a lot of money for. And in most cases it will turn out to be the kind of stain that can never be removed. But I might go on trying to wear the item of clothing anyway—hoping to hide the stain behind a pin or a scarf. Why? Because I'm THE MERR and that's the way I do things. And if you have a problem with that, well—that's your problem. Don't eat with me.

"I have no use for the old buzzards who try to tie me down with their rules and regulations. When I hear the call of the open road, sometimes I'll just get into my car, the radio blasting, the empty cans rattling around on the floor—my dog sitting beside me getting his light brown hair all over every single item of clothing I'm wearing—and I'll just barrel right on through a yellow light even though I know it's actually borderline legal. And I'll drive on into the sunset, hoping that this won't be one of the days when my dog will suddenly have to throw up. After all, he only does it about half of the time—not a high enough percentage for me to stop inviting him to come along altogether. Because I'm THE MERR. And these are the kinds of risks I am willing to take. It's just part of the way I live life on my own terms.

"Like the way I'll sometimes stay up until three or four in the morning, just worrying and fretting about bad scary things over which I have absolutely no control. And then when I do finally fall asleep it will be about five minutes before I have to get up so I'll be a wreck the rest of the day. Because I'm THE MERR. And that's just the way I do things."

Somehow it doesn't sound the same coming from a girl.

Afterword: How was I to know the impact my theory would have on the world at large? Just months after I wrote this piece, Madonna went on to break the sexist stereotype by being the first public woman to be as proud of her adolescent behavior as any football player, striking another important blow for parity of the sexes.

12,000 SQUARE FEET OF FUN

I guess one of the really great things about living in Los Angeles is that you're only a three-hour drive from a whole other country. I say this kind of tentatively because I've lived here on and off for ten years and have never actually made the drive across the border. Plus, when I mentioned my intentions to do so to my so-called friends, they all came up with excuses as to why they couldn't join me. Everyone did warn me, however, of the reasons to buy Mexican auto insurance, which is why I left my car in a big parking lot north of the border and headed into Tijuana on foot.

After passing through a turnstile into a dank cement corridor, the observant pedestrian immediately notices that all the garbage cans are labeled PRODUTSA. Voilà! Just like magic! You're in a whole other country! (But I probably shouldn't overstate the "magic" part of the experience, because the most magical thing about the cement corridor down which you find yourself strolling is a little stand selling Fresh Baja Shrimp Cocktails—a proposition that seems less than completely appealing, for the same reason that fresh shrimp never look all that good on sale at the bus depot.)

At this point, the pedestrian may select from a bevy of variously priced cab rides. I pick a $3 ride with a white-haired man in a pin-striped suit who looks like Cesar Romero would look after recovering from a debilitating illness. He drops me off in lovely midtown Tijuana, in front of Woolworth de Mexico, where a big sign proclaims EVERYONE'S FAVORITE! PIE À LA MODE! Inside at the lunch counter are those four elderly white people Woolworth apparently keeps on retainer and sends from town to town, paying them handsomely to sit and drink coffee.

Ah, Tijuana, where on every corner you can be photographed with a burro that someone has painted to look like a zebra. Tijuana, with its multitude of stores and stalls and arcades where you can purchase inexpensive items of no particular value or use. Like those jumbo-size paintings on velvet of Eddie Murphy and Prince and Madonna. A guy tells me they cost "$68 with the frame, or . . . how much you feel you'd like to spend, lady?" thus opening up a philosophical mind-bender similar to the one about the tree that falls in the forest and may or may not make a sound. What *is* the proper price to pay for a painting on velvet of Eddie Murphy? Pondering this, I move on to a giant bin of brightly colored automatic switchblades, which appear to be a good buy at $2.99 apiece, although I can't be too sure because I've never priced automatic switchblades before. (But I do purchase a dozen because it occurs to me they'll make awfully good stocking stuffers. And by the way, Tijuana is definitely *the* place for all your hideous-marionette needs. At no more than $2.50 apiece, they're an excellent buy.)

I exit this store and enter another one, and then exit and enter a series of stores so identical that I suspect the Tijuana Chamber of Commerce is trying to make me feel as though I am going insane, much as the guy did to his wife in the movie *Gaslight*. And out in front of each store there appears to be the same guy calling out to me, "Lady! This is the place!"

I find myself following a blond kid of about seventeen dressed in tan shorts and flip-flops. "She said she'd do *anything*," I hear him telling his demographically similar buddy. "*Really?* That's what she *said?*" the buddy replies as they both stop in front of a store window. "Those bongs are so rad. My parents got one just like that." We all walk in, past a large display of "pre-Columbian art" for $9.95. Inside the store I see two identically dressed identical twins (female) in their early sixties, each purchasing a bottle of Anaïs Anaïs. In the back of the store, just inches from the largest grouping of ceramic Little Bo Peeps I have ever seen, are clusters of pasty-faced Americans eating at dingy tables. And in the center of the store is a sign with an arrow indicating a descending flight of stairs and proclaiming 12,000 SQUARE FEET OF FUN! At the base of the stairs is a door, and from behind it comes the piercing shriek of gym whis-

WHAT THE DOGS HAVE TAUGHT ME

tles, my first acquaintance with "poppers"—a Tijuana custom wherein a restaurant patron has straight tequila poured into his or her mouth by a jovial waiter who is also blowing a whistle.

I am the sort of person who feels uncomfortable eating alone in a restaurant, and I've never been around more than 8,000 square feet of fun before, so as I begin my afternoon of solitary bar-hopping in Tijuana I realize I am taking some kind of significant developmental leap (although I've still not exactly determined in which direction). Many of the patio/restaurant/bar hangouts I visit are on sunlit rooftops and seem to have their fair share of guys who look like Jim McMahon or Bruce Willis on a bender. Everywhere, Tiffany-style disco music blares and clusters of people lean toward one another and act stupid while someone else takes their picture. I sit down next to a table full of blond girls who could model for a painting that would be called *The Three Ages of Rue McClanahan*. When the waiter comes over to inflict the dreaded poppers, one of them giggles too hard and gets her shot of tequila right in the eye.

Nearby, a Bruce Willis and a Jim McMahon good-naturedly agree to dance with two notably older ladies who make me feel embarrassed for them by their very big, self-conscious I'm-sure-a-lively-older-gal-aren't-I? dance movements.

As far as I can tell, I am the only unaccompanied person of either sex in all of Tijuana's bars. At the Tequila Circus, however, some of the chairs are molded plastic clowns adorned with horrifically bright, smiling faces, so a single gal like me can appear to be enjoying a glass of beer on the

••••••••••••••••••••••

142

lap of a psychotic circus performer. Across the street, People's: The Happiness and Joy Disco is done in a neo-Flintstonian motif. DANCE BACK ON TIME says the flashing sign as people I suspect might be shills try to encourage others to participate by boogying their brains out on the dance floor. This, by the way, is what happens when you accumulate some time in Tijuana—you begin to get a very definite sense that things are not at all what they seem.

Downstairs at the extremely crowded Tijuana Tilly's I am reunited with my friends the multiple blond girls—each of whom is now dancing seductively with one of a matching set of suave black dudes. I've heard it said that you can tell if a person is good in bed by the way he or she behaves on the dance floor. Not being a dancer myself (and quite frankly, never having dated anyone who was), I cannot confirm or deny the validity of this theory, but if we presume it to be true, the three blond girls have met up with the only dancers in Tijuana who definitely do *not* have a sexual dysfunction.

By now the harsh light of the late Sunday afternoon sun has made these "fun" college kids sucking down their shots of tequila look like the tired middle-aged businessmen and women they are destined to become. So I head back to the street to catch a cab. On my way I pass a storefront that says MARRIAGES AND DIVORCES. "May I help you, lady?" asks a guy out front as I take a peek inside. "No, I'm just looking," I say. "Want to get married? Let's get married," he suggests, and as flattered as I am, I realize it's time to head home.

Taking one last pass through the stores, I notice with

pleasure that whips are on sale for only $11.95, which I think is a darn good price, although I'm not sure because I've never priced any whips stateside (however, I do go ahead and purchase half a dozen since I *know* these will make darn good stocking stuffers.)

Talk about inflation! My taxi driver tells me the ride back to the cement corridor will cost *five* dollars! Even though I'm not the sort of person who likes to barter for things, I do manage to get him down to three. But then when I get out of the car goofiness overtakes me and I decide to give him five anyway. Okay, I'm an idiot, but I figure he has to keep driving around Tijuana while I get to go home. Which is exactly what I did.

A Dog Is a Dog Is a Dog

For months now I have been living in dog adoption hell. I sure hope I'm not going to be a permanent resident.

As anyone who has ever read more than two pieces of my work has probably noticed, I have kind of a dog fixation. Which I guess made it all the worse this past Thanksgiving when I lost my remaining dog. Well, I didn't really *lose* him. I *know* where he is. He's dead of a toxic overdose of ham.

Yes, you read correctly. My boy was killed by a house sitter who stupidly left about half a Honey Baked Ham in dog-stealing proximity. Once you know that toxic levels of fat in a prepared ham can destroy the pancreas, liver and kidneys of a seventy-five-pound dog, that ad featuring a smiling, tuxedoed O. J. Simpson holding up a giant silver serving tray of the stuff suddenly looks like a still from *Nightmare on Elm Street*.

I guess holiday gluttony was one weakness that both my dogs had in common. A few years back, my older dog, Bob, stole and consumed a ten-pound frozen turkey. Luckily for him, turkey has a very low fat content, and the worst side effect he suffered was the short-term embarrassment of looking briefly like a medium-size sofa bed.

Still, I was not at all prepared for Stan's death. He was in good health when I went away for Thanksgiving. And dead when I returned. It was the first time I had ever spent a minute in my house without him.

My life with Stan began when I realized that Bob didn't bark when people came into my yard. Only squirrels. I took some comfort in the fact that I was covered if a psycho dressed in a squirrel suit broke into my house, but I decided to bring in a backup line of defense. So I went to the pound and, in about fifteen seconds, plucked Stan off death row. He was the shyest, saddest-looking dog in a giant cage full of future dead guys. He also had a pair of ears on him that could have carried him airborne.

I think I selected him so quickly because his passive-aggressive approach broadcast the phrase "Rescue Me" louder than the energetic, friendlier efforts of all his cell mates. I had not yet realized that I was using the same method to select dogs that I was using to select men—with some of the same problematic results. Eventually Stan turned out to have uncontrollable homicidal urges toward others of his species. How often has a date of mine been ruined by much the same thing?

A Dog Is a Dog Is a Dog

Stan followed me everywhere, seeming to be operating with the mentality of someone who had either been abandoned or gotten badly lost and who was *not* going to make that mistake again. When I got into my pool to swim laps, he jumped in after me. From that point on he *never* let me out of his sight if he could help it. Day or night, even when I went into the bathroom, I could always count on the fact that Stan would be standing somewhere nearby, *staring* at me as though he felt something *good* was going to happen. This was his trademark. It always made me feel guilty because in most cases I knew damn well that nothing particularly good had been planned.

And so I had to live with the constant knowledge that I was continually letting him down. If I reached for a Kleenex, Stan would jump to his feet, certain that this was the first move in a potentially thrilling chain of events. He had an abiding belief that every action in this world might eventually lead to food or ball. In fact, he made this so clear to me that a fair percentage of the time I did try to follow up whatever I was doing with a little food or ball. Happily, he died without ever having learned the cruel truth that taking out the garbage or opening up the sock drawer does not *necessarily* signal any dog activity.

To his credit, Stan was an excellent ball player. Whereas Bob used to play "Catch the ball and eat it," Stan preferred "Double Dog Ball," in which two balls are put into play at all times, the one in the mouth being released at the same time that the one in the hand hits the air. This game could go on indefinitely—in fact, the more indefinitely the better. And because he was so enthusiastic in his playing, I generally chose to overlook the fact that he almost always took a dump on the dog ball field, during the third inning, with the ball still in his mouth. Anyone who has ever played this game will tell you that ordinarily this is an automatic out.

Also, thanks to Stan, I developed a certain confidence about my sloppy eating habits, secure in the knowledge that any food accidentally dropped onto the lower half of the room would instantaneously become his property. And because I was expected to give him a substantial portion of everything I was eating, I never really had to worry about consuming too many calories. Of course this was often just one more way in which I was a source of disappointment to him, since all he'd wind up with was a portion of some dumb salad. He'd eat it, but he wasn't happy about it. I bet the day that Honey Baked Ham turned up at my house must have seemed to him like some kind of answered prayer.

When he died, I sobbed for a couple of days, then everyone advised me to get "out there" and find myself a new dog. On day one of my search I called a series of ads from the *Los Angeles Times* that turned out to have been placed by a variety of kind ladies who feel compelled to rescue strays and then to attempt to find people to adopt them. This sounded like some kind of scam to me until I visited the suburban residence of a fiftyish Japanese lady who had two dogs in her front yard, two dogs in her backyard, one in her garage, five in her house and one in her station wagon. Since I had no automatic instinct about which of them to take, I decided not to rush things and left to think it over.

The next day on my way home from work I stopped by

the animal shelter nearest to my home and met dozens of other dogs, all cute. All potentially mine.

Overwhelmed again, I headed home alone. In the days that followed I repeated this behavior on a daily basis. Plus I added a way to confuse myself even further—I began taking some of the candidates out to a special yard to see if we had any "chemistry." That was when I learned that, though a dog may nuzzle you through the cage, when he is released from a kennel situation, he can offer you, at best, the kind of behavior I used to get from my own dogs when they were finally released from the vet. They would rush right on past in a sort of dog tornado, ignoring me totally in a mad dash to get the hell out. As depressing as it always was to receive that treatment from a beloved family pet, to have a strange dog treat you that way is even more peculiar. Not only does no chemistry occur, it is hard not to worry that maybe this new dog hates your guts. Anyway, after these experiences I decided to go home and think about it.

Then I paid a visit to something called the Pet Adoption Fund, in the San Fernando Valley, a large kennel facility where a lot of kind ladies board about 300 different dogs and cats that they have rescued. Walking past cage after cage of candidates I felt like a member of the parole board meeting thousands of eligible prisoners. Dog after dog would scream to me.

"I'm a big, dumb guy. Take me home and I'll kiss you, then eat all your furniture."

"I'm more sedate, but I'm kind of an older guy. I don't know you and I'm not sure I like you."

"I *love* you. Here, watch me make this dog face. See? Check it out. No one can resist it."

They were *all* going a million miles an hour.

That was the day it occurred to me that what I was actually looking for, in their faces, was the face of *my* dog. I was looking for that familiar stare that already knew me, already knew how to live with me and could come home and fit in and put things back the way they were. Which is why that was also the day I decided to knock off looking for a while. Because the reality is that there are *millions* of dogs who could be completely right for me. One thing you would have had to say about my two dogs was that they could easily be classified as "generic." But in the decades we spent together they each became so completely lovable and unique that each was irreplaceable. And in a way their very randomness makes the new selection process tougher. How in the world do I figure out which dog to save? I guess one day I'll just show up at one of these facilities and point and say, "That one." And then I'll have my new dog.

Ninety-eight percent of the dogs I meet are probably perfect. The whole key is that somehow *I* have to be ready.

THE DAY
I TURNED SARCASTIC

On January 1, 1959, these immortal words were recorded: "Dear Diary. Today the weather was not too nice. Little Bruce came over and got bitten by a slug. We ate hamburgers on the grill. Now it is 1959. Sincerely, Merrill." I was nine years old, and it was the beginning of an era. Well, maybe not an *era*, but it *was* the beginning of my close relationship with my diary.

It is a strangely pleasurable thing to read your own words from widely varying periods and phases of your life. You can hear not just how you thought but how you sounded at the moment you were thinking it. It's so much clearer and more specific than when your memory plays it back.

For instance, these days my brother and I are good friends, but this was not the case on January 22, 1959, when my rage moved me to scrawl in black India ink, "Today is Glenn's party, and he does not want me to come. He is a

•••••••••••••••••••••••

151

very greedy boy. When it was my birthday party he ate with the girls and played all the games and everything. And now it is his party and he says that I have to eat at a separate table from them and that I can't even talk to the boys, let alone play the games. I wont stand for it. I'll go to Jill's house where I'm welcome. Who needs his stinky party anyway." I can still vaguely remember the anger, but I would never have imagined it in those terms. It's been a while since I used the word *stinky* as effectively.

Part of the fun of reading about your own past is to chart your growth. On March 26, 1959, after viewing *The Story of Menstruation* with the rest of Girl Scout Troop 511, I had the following comments to make: "It was interesting. I decided that I would not wear lipstick or makeup until I was at least in my twenties. In fact, I might never wear it." On January 8, 1960, I amended that resolution slightly: "I decided that I wasn't going to wait until eighteen to wear lipstick but that I would wear it when fourteen." Then on June 1, 1960, "I decided that I am not going to wait until I am fourteen to wear lipstick but would wear it when I'm thirteen." And *then*, undated, but just a couple of pages later, "I decided that I wouldn't wait until thirteen to wear lipstick but would wear it when I go out to dinner or something at twelve."

It's a good thing I didn't have access to any sort of time-travel mechanism or I might have kept this lipstick rumination up indefinitely. It was hardly prophetic, anyway, since I didn't really get around to the whole lipstick thing until somewhere in my thirties.

The Day I Turned Sarcastic

Recently I found myself leafing through these early volumes in an attempt to discover the primitive roots of my need for self-expression. Self-expression was not the original motive. What fascinated me initially about diaries was the fact that these small, plastic-coated volumes decorated with drawings of teenage girls came equipped with a *lock* and a *key*. These temporarily kept safe from the prying eyes of family and strangers the sanctity of such top secret passages as "January 24, 1959. Went to school. At night I watched *77 Sunset Strip*. It was real good. 'Kookie' (Ed [*sic*] Byrnes) went skin diving." Or "February 28, 1959. After piano lessons we went to the Grand Union where Jim Dooley [a local TV personality] was. He came in a helicopter. Mr. Moke [a monkey] and his trainer came also. Mr. Moke did some tricks and we all got free Jim Dooley potato chips (ugg). I got Jim Dooley's autograph. He looks much much older in person."

Some of the entries were a little more controversial. On March 7: "I had a piano recital and did terrible. Miss Clemson gave me one day notice and told me to play 'Wheatlands.' Then the next day, which was the recital, she told me I had to play 'Waltz of the Flowers' AND 'Wheatlands.' I did awful on 'Waltz of the Flowers.' I hate her so much I feel like puking just at the sight of her."

The idea of the diary as a locked document only lasted until I discovered that every diary known to mankind was operated by the same key. And, what was worse, any bobby pin or scissor point could do the trick as well. That's how the idea of locking things up tight became secondary to a new motive—gaining a readership. Suddenly I was dropping asides to "whoever is reading this" or an invisible "you" (as in, "In case you want to know").

Seldom has the birth of a writer been so specifically documented. For instance, I now know that January 21, 1960, can be hailed as "The Day I Turned Sarcastic." The occasion was a Girl Scout Troop 511 rehearsal of the song selected by the troop leader as the one that would be performed at a countywide jamboree. "Linda Andrew found it in one of her baby piano books and we go around in a circle stamping our feet while we sing it. It's called 'Dance with Us, Sing with Us, Gretchen and Hans,' and we had to practice it over and over and over because *it's so hard to learn*, HA HA!"

It's probably significant that this kind of writerly awareness began to occur during the year when I first became sensitive about being treated like a child (read: chump), as seen in the entry for April 21, 1960, when "Mrs. Edwards was our teacher because Mr. Wilson had to go to a convention. She must have thought we were two-year-olds because she made us play 'Did you ever see a Lassie, a Lassie, a Lassie.' We were *DISGUSTED*."

This was also the time that I began my first misguided attempts at trying to interact in an appealing way with members of the opposite sex (an area in which to date I have made only the most marginal progress). On May 26, 1960, "I drew a picture on a piece of paper and wrote 'To Wayne; Roses are red, violets are blue. I killed my dog cause he looked like you' and then I left the note on his bicycle." At the bottom of the page, I added wistfully, "I wonder if he found it," as clueless then as to why verbal abuse may not be an effective come-on with guys as I was the other day when it fell through for me again for the hundred-thousandth time.

My biographers will want to make special note of July 15, 1960, which seems to mark the beginning of what can loosely be construed as some kind of a general world view. That was the day when I wrote, "Stayed home again. Still have a stuffed nose. In the evening the Democratic Convention nominated some guys for president."

The following year's events must remain shrouded in mystery, until the "lost writings of 1961" surface. But by 1962, I had ripened considerably, as a person as well as a journalist. And now I was pretty consistently addressing the proceedings to some kind of theoretical "you," as seen on January 1, when "my mother caught me reading Daddy's sexy desk calendar and took it away. It's unfit reading for a twelve-year-old, or so she says. I'll get it again though. Dont *you* worry."

The desire to get my message out to some kind of an audience was becoming more urgent—even if the message itself was still pretty dopey. On January 4, I phoned in a comment to the WFUN Radio newscast *and* diligently made a diary entry to record it for the ages. "In the news they talked about how a woman was complaining about the Coppertone billboard where they have the little girl with her butt exposed," I explained. "They wanted public opinions, so I called in and they played my comment at 7, 8 and again at 10. They called it a comment from a teenager. I said,

'With so many important things to criticize in the world I think this lady should use her voice to criticize more important things instead of picking on what I think is a cute ad. I wonder what she would have done if the little girl had been a grown woman.' " Now, I actually have no idea what I meant by that comment. Perhaps I was trying to say that we should all be grateful the ad was not much worse. Whatever it meant, this was the first documented moment of my ability to understand "the sound bite." Also to say nothing much succinctly.

Which brings us to the crux of the matter. Not long afterward I began to come under the influence of *The Diary of Anne Frank*. It was, to my teen eyes, less an account of the horror and tragedy of the Holocaust than an example of a girl my own age who had really done well in the diary game.

Suddenly I knew that I was going to have to roll out some big guns if I wanted to attract a readership throughout the ages, the way Anne Frank had, because I had not been given the gift of a tragic personal life to work with. Which is why, suddenly, my Month at a Glance highlight summaries began to read as follows:

September 13—Had my braces removed

September 17—Got a retainer

End of September sometime—A lot of trouble at U. of Miss. when Negro James Meredith tried to enter. Rioting. He got in though.

October 1—Lois's party

October 2—Candy's party

THE DAY I TURNED SARCASTIC

October 3—Walter Schirra made a sixth orbital flight. It was very successful and he returned nine hours later in good health and spirits.

But all this was just a prelude to the glorious day of October 22, when, through the grace of God, I was handed the first significant world event I could really milk diarywise. October 22 was the beginning of the Cuban missile crisis, and we were living in Miami. At last, something nearby of greater theatricality than my brother's bad behavior! Oh sure, I was able to generate a little thirteen-year-old angst here and there with a few "I'm a social outcast. Everyone is going to the dance except me"-type musings, but they were nothing compared to this first visitation of a national nightmare right in my own backyard (sort of). The entries for October 22 and 23 read: "Turned in our home ec. notebooks. In the afternoon President Kennedy made a public address. He spoke of the fastly being erected USSR missile bases in Cuba and how this could not be tolerated. He said that a quarantine would begin around Cuba and all ships would be checked for offensive weapons. Four Russian ships are on their way. There's a possibility that this may be the last Tuesday I'll ever live through. The next forty-eight hours will decide whether there will be peace or war. I feel like crying but I can't I dont want to die. There's so much out of life I've never experienced. I'll never complete my education or fall in love or be married and have children. I'll never see the rest of the world. God. I'm only thirteen and there's still so much ahead. I don't want to die." Never mind that the entry the next night was business as usual.

"Went to Andi's party," I wrote. "The highlight of the whole thing was a scavenger hunt."

Never mind that twenty-seven years later I have made good on only *one* of my top five reasons for living through the Cuban missile crisis. For at least one fabulous day, global politics and international strife had done a little something on my behalf. And so I was able to find a small measure of diary fulfillment, however short-lived.

By 1963 I had entirely given up on the idea of incorporating world events into my diaries. I was hard at work on my first and only novel. My influence had changed from Anne Frank to Holden Caulfield, and so was born 125 pages in which I detailed, amid plenty of casual swearing, my acute ability to distinguish the phonies from the real people. Entitled *The Cheese Stands Alone*, this remains such an intensely embarrassing piece of work that I think I'll just go ahead and end right here.

QUEEN FOR A DAY

I have long harbored a fear that the part of my brain in charge of instincts about female glamor and related topics was incorrectly assembled at the plant. I'm referring to the part that controls such things as the slow exhalation of smoke while sipping a brandy; the part that turns laughter sexy and leaves out the snorts and the spitting; and the part that allows you to look elegant while you eat a meal and also not wind up with bread crumbs in your bangs. It began to seem unfair to me that some *men* seem to know more about being a girl than I do. Which made me wonder about those human beings for whom both sexes come easily, when I am still having trouble getting the rules right on *one*. So I thought I'd find out the difference between playing a woman and playing a man from the folks who regularly do them both.

"When I first started applying makeup, I wasn't very good

at it," Scott tells me, "but a couple of the kids here took me aside and totally revamped me." Scott is a skinny pale white guy of thirty who is diligently applying layer after layer of magenta and violet eye shadow. He is seated at a makeup mirror in a large dressing room shared by the guys who perform in the regular drag show at the Queen Mary near Los Angeles. "The difference between me as a man and me as a woman is there is no difference. I'm me," he says. This is hard to believe when he goes into action on stage. In the course of the show he appears in one sexy, glamorous gown-and-wig combo after another, looking like an assortment of women from *Knots Landing*. He circulates through the darkened room full of tables, shimmying, dancing, vamping, and stopping to flirt with the male half of the mostly straight audience. "There's no difference, because I don't think of it as a man or a woman," he says, "but when you put on a certain hat, the full hair, a dress—you just change in some way." He is, of course, describing a change with which I am not familiar.

"It's the eyelashes," Marvin tells me. "When I put them on, I feel the transformation beginning." Seated at another mirror across the room, Marvin is a sweet, sad-eyed, over-weight man in his mid-thirties. "The most ridiculous thing is the shoes," he says, pointing to a several-tiered tray full of spiked heels. As we continue to talk, he expresses concern for the fact that he is quite heavy. But when he hits the stage, he really gets around, pudgy or no. He's a ball of energy, dressed in a lace tunic, fingerless gloves, a futuristic wig, and a headband, as he danced and lip-syncs "Jump" in lieu of all three Pointer Sisters. "It's like I do this for the big ladies who come in," he says, "because as a big woman I look very good. And if *I* can, there's no reason they have to sit home and be ashamed of who they are." (Oddly enough, though Marvin mentions that his weight restricts him from wearing the kind of men's clothes he would like to wear, he is at a loss to explain why he cannot do for the big men what he feels he does for the big ladies.)

"Really, darling, pantyhose do change the attitude," Gypsy tells me at lunch the next day while I look at a publicity photo of him as the emcee at the La Cage Aux Folles nightclub. Gypsy, who's six foot one in heels, says he's a size ten dress. In this photo he is wearing an outfit he describes as "the mother of the Woodland Hills bar mitzvah boy trying to impress younger relatives with less money." (Later that night at La Cage, he is wearing a hot-pink skirt hiked up under his armpits, creating an effect that could be called, I guess, an off-the-shoulder mini muu-muu.) "Actually, I feel more feminine out of all that. Being with you I feel more like a woman than I do on stage," he tells me in a confiding tone, and I take it as a compliment, because not every woman can make a man feel more like a woman just by sharing a table with him at lunch.

"Being a man or being a woman is really located some-where between your ears," he says. "But what happens," I want to know, "when you cross the line from one sex to the other? What part of your behavior do you change when you want to feel more feminine?"

"I shut up. Women have a tendency to get quiet when a

gorgeous guy walks by. Straight men go like this: 'Hey look at that hot chick,' " he says, changing his voice to that of a construction worker and elbowing at the air. "Emotionally I'm a woman." But later at La Cage, I watch Gypsy spring into action when a gorgeous guy comes in with a female companion. "Hey you!" Gypsy shouts across a crowded room. "Yes, you! You left your underwear on my living room floor last night! The dog is going crazy! The maid is going berserk! The neighbors won't speak to me! And I just don't care!" The object of all this attention barely moves an eyebrow—the kind of response that not many women would live through. Although, come to think of it I have never met a woman brave enough to scream a come-on to a stranger across a bar. But Gypsy is nonplussed. "That guy would be the *worst* date," he whispers to me. "I'm the only woman who could survive a date like that. And only because I'm a guy."

At lunch, we'd discussed the difference between the sexes. "Femininity means something soft and gentle," he told me. "That's why I turned gay. Straight men think if you're gentle and sweet you should also say yes constantly. I wasn't about to be subservient."

"But you don't think *all* straight men need to have people be subservient to them, do you?" I ask, inexplicably defending a type of guy I'm not sure I've ever met myself.

"Absolutely," says Gypsy. "Honey, I know how screwed up men are, because I used to *be* one. Men are rats. *I* was a rat. I thought I was more powerful because it was *my* thing sticking in her. She had *nothing* sticking in me."

"So," I say, mulling this over. "You think that *single act* defines the difference between men and women?"

"You think it doesn't?" he says incredulously. "My dear! I better educate you!"

A waiter arrives at our table, and Gypsy, the man, orders for us. "She's going to have the ricky dicky doo salad," he tells the guy, pointing to a "salad rustica" on the menu, "and I'll have this kicky micky with cheese."

The topic shifts to the glory days of his marriage. "My ex-wife did nothing but lay on her ass and complain," he tells me. "It's girls like her who make girls like me." I try to digest that. "And what does that mean?" I ask.

"What does that mean?" he says in astonishment, rolling his eyes to the heavens. "Honey, how can a brilliant girl like you know nothing? That's all you've said all afternoon! 'I know nothing! I understand nothing!' Listen, a man can throw my legs up in the air and throw your legs up in the air, and we're in the same position, right? But *my* thoughts are a lot different than *yours*. Because I know where he's coming from. I know that's all he really wants. Because I'm a man. A woman will lie to herself. A woman thinks he wants much more." Now this part is starting to sound familiar.

Given all this sexual traversing, I am curious to know which sex those who have sampled both venues would pick if they could start over again. Marvin and Scott assure me that, out of drag, they would rather be men. Gypsy agrees. "No way would I want to *be* a woman," he says. "Men have no responsibility. Women are not free. Even the ones who make $300,000 a year. They're not free. They're free until they take their pantyhose down, dear. Then I have news for you. They're not free anymore. I knew the minute you walked in that door, she's got all kinds of questions about herself. But if she thinks she can get any answers from me, she's crazy." Scott has different parting advice. "Redo your eyebrows," he tells me. "Those are hideous."

And so we leave the twilight world of female impersonation, where folks can glide easily from one sex back to another. As we wave good-bye, I realize there is something I have learned: next time I need to attend a formal social event, I'll just hire Scott to impersonate me. Then people can watch him toss his hair to catch the light and slink around in lamé and laugh a smoky laugh, and they'll think, *She's finally got it together.*

HOME ALONE

The other night I ate a pack of frozen hors d'oeuvres for dinner: three weenie rolls, two egg rolls, three potato puffs and three air-filled triangular things. When I confided this information to a friend, she remarked, "Well, that's the kind of thing you can do only when your life is completely unobserved."

This is the first extended period of time that I have lived alone. By "alone" I mean without humans, because, except for a few weeks, I have always had dogs (and dogs are no help at all when it comes to goofy behavior. In most instances they only encourage it). Which brings me to my point: When you live alone you are apt to turn into the silliest version of yourself, simply because there is no one around to stop you.

When you live with your parents, you are expected to play by their rules, no matter how hip or evolved your folks might pretend to be. And when you live with a man—I don't need to tell you how it works when you live with a man, do I? After a lifetime of living both with parents and with men, I am only too well acquainted with what have erroneously been referred to as my "annoying habits." The question is, Are your habits still annoying if there is no one around to say he or she is pissed off? And of course the answer comes back a resounding "No! No! A thousand times no!" It's just like magic. When you live by yourself, all your annoying habits are *gone!!*

Which is not to say that living alone is something to strive for. Quite frankly, several things about it are not too appealing. It can be lonely and boring. There's no one around to whine to. Plus, you have to lift those enormous containers of bottled water all by yourself. I once stayed in a relationship almost a year past its due date just to avoid confronting the issue of the giant bottles of water.

The good part is that these circumstances force you to learn to do stuff you might otherwise have avoided entirely, like finding out where the circuit breakers are and how to turn off the water at its source. Or how to eat alone in a restaurant without making a face that continuously says, "The person who is meeting me here should have been here by now. I wonder what in the world is keeping him or her!"

When you live alone you find yourself getting both very brave and very stupid. There's no one to comment when you play one cut from an album 300 times in a row. Or rent a movie and replay it during the cute guys. You can go *whole days* without turning the television on at all (cheerfully ignoring those important hours of stock-car racing from Daytona!). Finally, there's the real plus: When you live by yourself you don't have to worry that you're not getting enough fats and sugars in your diet.

The bad part is that it's possible, by indulging your whims, to turn into a caricature of yourself. There is a point at which the good side of living alone and the bad side of living alone converge and become one. For instance, one of the good things is that you can relax and spend the whole day looking like a pig if you want to. And one of the bad things is that you can catch a glimpse of yourself in the mirror and realize that you have just spent the whole day looking like a pig. This is a phenomenon I call the Fish Table Principle, so named because when you live by yourself, you can go ahead and buy a table that looks like a fish without fear of reprisal. But then you have to go through life pretending to enjoy living with a table that looks like a fish.

So we see that this whole living alone business is a mixed bag. But having done it for the past couple of years, I feel I must caution the neophyte to avoid one danger area right from the start. I refer to the reading of articles in women's magazines, like *Cosmopolitan*, that purport to give advice on living by yourself with flair. They almost always involve "pampering yourself," which generally boils down to "treat yourself to a bubble bath!" Then there's the old "cooking a fabulous dinner for one, using the good china and the good silver" technique. (Right away making the dangerous assumption that you may have some of each.)

When I first started living alone, I used to scour these articles. Quickly they became a source of real irritation.

The truth is that a lot of women end up living alone as a result of troublesome circumstances. These women, like me, have quite enough to worry about without the added stress of feeling they're not executing their daily rituals with sufficient style to please Helen Gurley Brown. So, let the *Cosmo* women lightly braise their short ribs and toss up a celeriac vinaigrette for one. Here are my alternative suggestions for the flakier, lazier woman who doesn't want to go to the store because it's too cold (or too hot) and anyway there's still half a box of Wheat Thins and a couple of beers in the fridge.

Merrill Presents Eight Things to Do When You Are Living Alone, Because Now There Is No One to Stop You

1. Dye your hair a lot of exotic colors that always fascinated you but you were too chicken to try. Then cut it all off, buy a really big hat, walk up to randomly selected people on the street, glare at them and say ferociously, "What exactly are you staring at?"

2. See if you can eat a full three-course dinner in your car before even leaving the supermarket parking lot. Be sure to use the good silver.

3. Test really unusual clothes for falling asleep in. While you're at it, why not try sleeping on a different edge of the bed every night?

4. Shave the dog, oil him, then sit next to him out in the yard and see who gets a good all-over tan first.

5. Take yourself out on a date! Make reservations at your favorite restaurant. At the table, try moving back and forth between two chairs as you find out where you're from and what your major was in college. Afterward, if you feel there's too much pressure on you to go right to bed, take out a can of Mace and spray yourself thoroughly.

6. One night cook yourself a dinner that includes lean meat/fish/poultry, leafy green or yellow vegetables and a starch!

7. Call up a radio psychologist under the pretense of needing some help, and when he or she says, "Turn your radio down," turn it *up!*

8. Call to get an appointment with the phone repair guy or someone from the gas or electric company. When they ask, "Will someone be home between 8:00 A.M. and 10:00 P.M.?" reply, "No, I live by myself and I work for a living. I can't be there for fourteen hours in a row." When they begin to tell you that they're sorry, they're very sorry, but unless someone is there from 8:00 A.M. to 10:00 P.M. there's nothing they can do to help you, tell them to please hold. Drive quickly to their place of employment, find them and threaten them with bodily harm from a blunt instrument. At your trial insist that "a jury of my peers" means "other single people who live alone." You'll be cleared of all charges and home playing the same cut on the album 300 times in a row in no time flat.

I, LEWIS

My name is Lewis, and it was initially my plan to live with Barbara Bush in the White House. But she was a no-show. So I came to live with Merrill Markoe instead. It was January 1991, and her previous dog, Stan, had died a couple months earlier from a toxic overdose of ham. None dare call it suicide.

I feel I should say at this point that I have found people pretty strange from the first, but this woman is nuts, and I mean that sincerely.

So anyway, I was about seven weeks old (which is like 150 of your years), and I go to sleep one night and the next day when I wake up I'm in solitary. I mean, I realized I was big for my age, but I'll be damned if I know what I did. One minute I'm being born. The next I'm a lifer. And I'm the youngest one in the joint. I don't know what stunt I pulled during my nap, but I think it was a doozy.

So I'm in the slammer and not much is happening. People stop by and stick their hands through the bars in my cell, and I gnaw on their fingers with my razor-sharp teeth until I draw blood or they cry out in pain. And that's about it for activity until day two, when this big gangly woman stops by. She's wearing jeans and she's got brown hair on her head and blond hair on her arms, so I figure she's a mixed breed. I'm leaning against the bars, biting her for as long as she can stand it—I'm getting very close to making a puncture wound—when I hear a lot of discussion, and the next thing I know, she springs me. She puts me on her lap and starts driving, which I know can't be very safe. At first I think maybe she's taking me to meet *Air Force One*. However, it begins to hit me that her car smells like dog vomit. Which makes me think she's not a Republican.

When we arrive at her house, right away I can't believe my eyes because *everywhere I look is a great place to go to the bathroom!!!* But already I'm thinking this woman has some serious mental problems, because every time I start to take a leak, she's in my face interrupting me. She's going, "No! No! No!" and trying to make me relocate *out in the yard!!!* I'm serious! In the dark! Or in the rain!!! Like it's the eleven hundreds. Suddenly I think I'm Olivia de Havilland in *The Snake Pit*.

The craziness doesn't end here. Now I find out that she doesn't want me to eat. I mean, I'm starving, I'm *teething*, and her place is like a big all-you-can-eat buffet. *Everywhere I look is edible stuff*. But when I try to take a mouthful she's in my face again. She doesn't want me to eat *anything*. Not clothes. Not nails. Not candles. Not door frames. Not *nothing*. It's like everything I know to be true about the world has suddenly shifted, and now every single idea that I have is a problem. As it happens, I've always prided myself on my original thinking. I'm an idea man. But suddenly this woman is telling me that *everything I do is wrong*.

I get the idea "Let's pull up the rug and eat the foam-rubber pad" and of course, no, we can't do that. So then I figure, "Let's eat all the wires wherever we find them attached to the wall," and that's no good. So then I think, "Let's find a pack of needles behind the bed and chew on them," and of course, there's something wrong with that too. And it doesn't even occur to her that the law of averages would dictate that *all* these ideas couldn't possibly be bad. That just maybe *she's* wrong occasionally.

Obviously, something else is going on here. I mean, it's more than a coincidence that she doesn't want me to pull up her plants *or* rip her upholstery *or* eat her books and magazines. It begins to dawn on me that I'm more than just a long, long way from the White House. I mean, not only do I not attend cabinet meetings, but I seem to be stuck in some kind of banana republic here, with her as the pack leader!! (And as far as I can tell, all she has in the way of qualifications is *height*.) It's not just the arbitrary restrictions; now when she leaves the house, she locks me up in the kitchen.

The first gate she puts up I can climb, no problem. Even though it's covered with wire mesh, I can just dead-drop to the floor. And so for at least that one brief shining moment

I am actually able to accomplish things that I can point to with pride. For instance, by the time she gets home that day I've not only dismantled and consumed most of a telephone, but I've also eaten over half of the paperback *Toxic Parents: Overcoming Their Hurtful Legacy and Reclaiming Your Life.*

Let's just say she's not impressed by this. I don't think she gets the message I'm trying to send her, either. Instead of looking within, she just hires a guy to make the gate more difficult to climb! So now when she goes out, I have no choice but to sit in the kitchen alone, surrounded by mysterious squeaking vinyl food replicas. I don't understand the full implications of that pork chop, but I do know it's the toughest, noisiest piece of meat with which I have ever had the misfortune to be imprisoned.

By now I've realized that this woman and I have very little in common, also that we seem to have a completely different relationship to every single thing in the universe. Give you an example. She's sitting on the bed, doing nothing, with a lap full of newspapers. So I decide to take the edge of one section and run around with it and then sit on it and shred it into tiny fragments. This breakthrough idea meets with the kind of reactionary response that has plagued all forward-thinking individuals throughout history. Galileo and Leonardo and Brian Bosworth come to mind. Of course she's yelling "No! No! No!" like her way is the *only* way. Let's all just fill our laps with papers and *sit* there. It's no wonder her last two dogs had eating disorders.

And then there are the shots. Then more shots. I won't

even tell you about them. It would sicken you. But at about week 16 the shots suddenly end and the walks begin. This is my first opportunity to build some equity in the neighborhood. I realize right off it's a smart idea to acquire as much beachfront property as possible, what with the recession and everything. But what surprises me is the effortless way in which I am permitted to annex several impressive pieces of property, not the least of which is Johnny Carson's tennis compound—a several-acre island parcel off a cul-de-sac about a half mile from my central residence. It takes me only about two weeks of saturation peeing to take full title.

I admit to being a little surprised that Carson didn't put up any kind of a fight at all. On the other hand, I don't know how much he uses the place these days. There's mushrooms growing on the southeast corner and a dead bird just slightly west, which I have never seen him even try to roll on.

At about this point in the Barbara Bush book, there's a big kiss-ass section with photos of Millie mingling with important government officials and celebrities. I was going to include a section like that in here, but frankly I found the whole thing pathetic. Sure, I could name-drop. I just don't feel the need. Why should I try to make myself sound more important by telling you that last weekend at the dog park in Laurel Canyon I sniffed Julia Roberts's big fat black dog's butt?

No, I refuse to resort to that kind of nonsense, because I happen to believe that some things matter more than having your picture taken sitting with Secretary of State George Shultz and Her Majesty Queen Noor of Jordan. Or French president François Mitterrand and Mrs. Yasuhiro Nakasone. That's why I have decided to close by sharing with you a part of my credo, which I hope you will value and cherish as I do.

My Credo

If you like something well enough to climb on it or kiss it, then don't you also owe it to yourself to eat it or destroy it? Can't you at least take the time to pick it up in your mouth and run with it as fast as you can from room to room until it drops? Or shred it into microscopic particles?

Because as we wander through this world, I think it is important not to lose sight of this amazing truth: *Everything* is potentially an entrée, if not also a side dish or an hors d'oeuvre. If you look at things properly, you'll come to realize that there's no need to wait for the dessert cart. Dessert is *everywhere*. Thank you.

HOUSE PITIFUL

Last weekend I went to Cincinnati for my brother's wedding, and I had a number of interesting experiences. I stayed in a hotel overrun with members of the conventioning International Gay Bowlers Organization (IGBO). I attended a street fair called the Taste of Cincinnati, where I was able to watch older members of the citizenry dance out of sync to the slowest version of "In the Mood" that I have ever heard performed in public. All this, plus the opportunity to witness my brother—whom I still recall as an adolescent standing in the doorway to my room, fluttering his eyelids and dangling his tongue while he turned my light on and off, on and off, on and off—share a genuinely heartfelt moment with his now-wife that made tears roll down my cheeks.

That was very moving, but I felt an equally intense reaction the next day when I visited my brother's cute little house and realized that even he is a better home decorator than I am. A guy who spent his early years stalking moving cars with a peashooter now knows how to have pillows made from fabric he bought, and build his own room dividers. While *I*, who should have the chromosomes for this sort of thing, continue to decorate rooms by lining up cheap plastic funny stuff on the shelves.

I have become increasingly concerned about my lack of instinct for home decorating. It stems from an even more unlikely shortcoming, given my gender, which is this: I have a real problem with shopping. No, no—it's not *that* problem. Mine is the opposite problem, which is that I never buy anything. I can spend hour after hour going through stores full of patio furniture and kitchenware and shoes and come home *emptyhanded* . . . and what makes it even more alarming is that I do this even after being paid!

There are things that I do buy, such as occasional sacks full of toys, magazines and gum. I also have a weakness for odd plastic items that come in a bubble pack and represent a soon-to-be-extinct cultural trend. But I'm not fanatical about them. I don't call myself "a collector." I buy these things simply because I find them funny. Then when I get home, I generally put them up on a shelf. And that is pretty much all I do in the way of decorating.

I never think of ideas like hanging nineteenth-century farm equipment from the ceiling. All my oxen yokes are back in the lower forty with the oxen. When I see those photos in *Architectural Digest* of rooms with a cluster of behemoth earthenware pots in one corner and maybe an empty aircraft section made into a planter, I am mightily impressed, but even if I wanted to steal the idea, I wouldn't know where to find a clay pot the size of a pony. And even if I saw such a pot on sale, I wouldn't be sure if $6,000 was a good price, or if I was being overcharged by $5,500.

Furthermore, I'm just not sure how I feel about having a handcrafted Navajo Indian ladder leaning against my living room wall. Is this a good idea, or just a passing fancy, like those bell-bottoms that we couldn't stop wearing in the Seventies? Such questions are more serious when it comes to home decor because you have to live with your purchases for all eternity. How do I know that a freestanding closet with three colors of peeling paint is an item I want to take with me to the grave?

About once a year the inadequacy of my efforts crashes over me like a tidal wave, usually after I get back from a visit to someone else's home. "Why didn't I think of re-upholstering my ottoman with my curtains?" I lament. "Why don't I *have* any curtains? Why didn't I think of *owning* an ottoman? And why haven't I filled the fireplace with fresh flowers?"

My brother has beautiful souvenirs from his world travels. He has ceramics from Greece and Egypt and handmade rugs from Jordan. He actually had a lamp made-to-order in Cyprus. I have a snow shaker from Bermuda, a snow shaker from Florence, snow shakers from Saint-Tropez and London. There's definitely something peculiar about me.

I did once decide to tackle my problem in a practical, orderly fashion, by hiring a decorator. This was a man who had selected unique and lovely items for some of my friends. My friends kept saying he was eccentric, but that didn't bother me because everyone I know is eccentric. I've wined with them, I've dined with them, I've slept with them . . . in fact I hardly know anyone who doesn't fit the category.

When the day came, I was fully prepared to meet a flamboyant guy wearing a boa and carrying a poodle, but not for the depressed fellow who came to my door. . . . He was unkempt and rumpled, and he sighed deeply enough to inhale every bit of usable air in a three-block radius. Then he shuffled to a chair where he collapsed into a boneless heap, chain-smoking. Lugubriously he gazed up at me and suggested items to beautify my home. That's how I got my thing that you hang your hats and coats on. By the time my dealings with him were over, I knew all about the ruins of his personal life, and I no longer had the desire to get up in the morning. After all, the sun is due to burn out, and the universe is going to implode. How cute does your home have to look to be ready for that? Not too many months later, I decided it was better to live without end tables than to lose the will to live. I fired him.

The topic of home decor remained unresolved until my brother's wedding. The sight of his house gave me such a shock that I rushed off to the Home Restoration and Remodeling Show at the Los Angeles Convention Center as soon as I got home. "Find out how to turn your home into a castle" was what the newspaper ad had said. The fact that I'd never given any real thought to living in a castle is probably just more of the sickness that has held me prisoner all these years. But here was a chance to "meet the wizards of home improvement," and the local TV personalities who were supposed to attend (presumably because they become fixtures in your home, even if they are about half as interesting to talk to as your coffee table).

The show turned out to be just a giant room full of those sections of the department store that I try to avoid. There were countless booths selling paneling, veneer, wrought-iron curlicues, doorknobs, handles and light switches—things that cause the sound of bees in my head. The buzzing grew louder as I tried to interact with the materials—actually to *look* at a book of molding patterns or bathroom fixtures. By the time I had reached "the decorating den," also known as "the colorful store that comes to your door" ("Our color van contains over 3,000 samples of drapes, carpets, wall coverings and upholstery"), I could no longer hear words but see only lips moving silently. At the Red Skelton clown-painting booth where I found myself focusing on paintings with names like *Lord 'elp Us* and *Timmy*, I began to imagine that I was the host of a brand new PBS show roughly based on the premise of *This Old House*, except that in *my* show I would painstakingly demonstrate my ability to take a home of considerable potential and raw natural beauty and turn it, bit by bit, increment by increment, into the duplicate of the lowest priced rooms at Motel 6.

And so I left, having purchased nothing at all, and feeling so discouraged that I got up early the next day and headed out to a prestigious shopping mall where many of my friends leave behind giant chunks of their salaries. And I am proud to report that, after hours and hours of surveying its contents—of looking through gadgets and crystal and lamps and cushions and sleepwear—I came home with a rubber stamp of a man sipping a cocktail and a molded plastic dinner roll with feet that walks when you wind it up. Both items were available in complementary shades of tan or beige so they go with everything in the room, which has never looked better.

Born Yesterday

In spite of the fact that I was born in the East and lived there for quite a few years (and by the way, East Coast girls *are* hip—I really dig those styles they wear), I am basically a California girl. Left to my own devices, I exercise regularly, often eat health foods and sometimes put lemon juice in my hair (of course, I sometimes put coleslaw in my hair too, but that's a story too horrible for these pages). I compulsively read local publications to stay current with trends that I kind of suspect are useless, but I'm never really sure. I mention this stuff to let you know that I am open to things, which is why all the ads in the back of the local weekly papers offering "past life regressions" have always held a certain mysterious allure. There are dozens of this kind of ad in the Southern California area, not even counting anything to do with Shirley MacLaine. My favorite ad is the one for a hypnotist who offers a variety of services; right under past life regressions is listed bust development. (I couldn't imagine going to him because, quite frankly, I was afraid to grow bigger breasts even in a past life under hypnosis with a strange man in the room.)

I. Past Lives. Day One: The Adventure Begins

Recently I began to inquire as to which past life regressions might be right for me. My attitude was as follows: I have been to Bermuda, therefore I believe in Bermuda. After I visit some past lives, then I'll believe in them too.

The ad in the back of the *Whole Earth Review* says, "Assoc. for Past-Life Research & Therapy, Inc.," and the area code indicates that it is about a three-hour drive from my house. But when I call, the woman who answers wants to know what geographical area would be most convenient. "What's your zip code?" she asks me. "I have hundreds of past life regressionists listed in Southern California." So I settle for one located in the industrial section of Marina Del Rey, in what turns out to be a tiny little office behind a boat supply store.

Inside, at an enormous desk, is Bettye Binder (B.A., Barnard, American Government; M.A., Columbia, Public Administration and American Government). Bettye is nothing if not sensible looking; the combination of her tightly coiffed hair and red lipstick gives her the appearance of a professor or librarian, which is probably why I am not moved to greater irreverent goofiness when she tells me about her 3-D hologram-style spontaneous memories of Indians who started trekking through the center of her home just a few weeks after she attended a lecture during which she sat near a man with whom she felt a "strong sense of familiarity." To make a long story short, it turns out they were Comanche Indians together in the 1700s. Then Bettye Binder became so absorbed in her past lives that she decided to go into them for a living.

"Are there any people who do not get regressed to anything?" I ask her. "No," she says, "*everyone* gets regressed. I've done, conservatively, 2,000 regressions, and in all of these, people have regressed back to *something* somewhere." But how will I know when I am really experiencing a past life and not just making one up? After all, I make up stuff for a living. Bettye assures me that what will take place does not come from imagination. "The meditative state allows you to get deep into the unconscious," she explains, "and block out the chatter, and as a result you get information that will surprise you. It will be very different from what you would get if you were writing a story."

Bettye asks what I would like to work on. For instance, some people have met someone who seemed strangely familiar. Not me—I sometimes have trouble recognizing even close relatives. And I'm plumb out of eerie experiences altogether, even though I once dated a guy who saved all his bakery numbers. So Bettye says I might work off something from the present. I suggest an exploration into my compulsive use of humor, and Bettye thinks that's a fine idea. "We're going to work on a past life connected to humor," she says as I lie down on a cot in the back of the office. Bettye sits down beside me on a straight-backed chair. "Close your eyes. I'll start the music."

WHAT THE DOGS HAVE TAUGHT ME

She turns on a cassette of some new age thing that sounds like randomly selected wind chimes, glass bells and flutes. Bettye begins to speak in a singsongy voice that reminds me of a nursery school teacher trying to calm the kids for nap time. She tells me to relax and "find a nice safe place to receive love and light and let go of negativity." She instructs me to slowly saturate myself in each of the colors of the rainbow and then to pull all the negativity out of me like taffy. Soon we are moving backward . . . backward . . . backward through time, and stepping into our past body as though it were a suit of clothes.

"Look around you," she says. "Who are you? No matter what you see or know, tell me what it is." The new age music hits a crescendo, and I am seeing . . . gray. It's the same gray I always see when I close my eyes. I feel just terrible. Okay, okay, maybe it's not just gray. Okay, "I'm seeing sky," I say, hoping to please. "Now look down at your past life feet," she tells me. "Are you wearing anything on your feet? *Just these dumb old past life shoes* is what I'm thinking. "I don't know," I say honestly. "Okay, move up your body. Tell me what you sense you're wearing." The new age flutes are honking and beeping. I'm getting nothing, but mumble, "Maybe like leotards." "Are you male or female?" she asks. "I don't really have a sense of myself," I confess. "You don't have to have a picture. Just trust whatever pops into your head," she says, and recaps what we have learned here so far.

"This is a past life connected with humor," Bettye repeats patiently. "You're in leotards, and you're walking now.

Where are you going?" she asks. "I don't know. I'm seeing a grayish color inside my eyelids," I answer. "What is there near you that is gray?" she asks me, trying to help. "Nothing," I answer. "The gray I see is just that kind of gray that is nothing." "The gray that is nothing," she repeats, making it sound like a lot more than I intended. "Walk to the gray that is nothing. Make it your friend. Feel it. Reach out and hug the gray. Give it a nice big hug." There is a clatter, and she turns the new age music over. "What is the gray saying to you?" she asks me soothingly. "What does the gray represent to you?" "Panic," I confess. "Panic because I'm not coming up with any past lives." "Don't fight it," she says. "Feel it. Relax! Permit yourself to be in those leotards. . . . Where are you going in those leotards?" she asks me. "Don't edit," she adds. I'm in Rome, circa 70 B.C., and I'm going to the invention of the Jazzercising class. Hey! There's Julius Caesar. Whoa! Look at that white boy do sit-ups! "I don't know," is what I actually say. "I'm going to bring you back, and let's talk again," she says.

I sense discouragement in her placid voice. "Come through your birth," she says, and I do my best. "Now you're five. You're a little girl having fun. What are you doing?" I decide I am going to do a nice job on *this* section at least. So I revive an old memory involving digging a hole in my parents' yard. "Really have fun digging that hole," she encourages me. "Dig in that hole just as long as you like. Are you having fun?" *Well, it's okay* is what I'm thinking. But even at five it was no week at Caesars Palace. "I guess it wasn't all *that* much fun," I confess. "I don't think you've had much fun *period*" is her parting remark. Whoa! Hurt me, mama!

II. Day Two: The Regression Continues

Feeling like a failure the next day, I drag my friend Carol down to the Hyatt hotel in Long Beach where we will attend "Carole Carbone's Past Life Odyssey Workshop." My friend Carol is a bright, funny woman whose weakness for new age crap is even bigger than mine. I have known her to consult more than once with a psychic nutritionist.

Carol and I take seats at one of the four fully occupied round tables in the meeting room. We are sitting with a bearded guy in his thirties who sells software and a very soft-spoken man in his forties who turns out to be a Honda dealer. We are joined by a chunky dark-haired woman who writes for a local weekly.

Now Carole Carbone takes the podium. An ordained metaphysical minister, she is perky and attractive in a Terry Cole-Whittaker kind of way. She explains to us matter-of-factly that we are going to experience several past lives, as well as see our own deaths, and will also go into the future to see ourselves a year from today. Plus there will be lunch and a number of bathroom breaks. Someone in the class asks if she should wear her glasses. It doesn't matter.

So we close our eyes and listen to a seven-minute tape of bits and pieces of music ranging from Gregorian chants to Alpine horn music. After the tape is finished, we go around the room and tell how the music made us feel. The chunky woman takes the first of many opportunities to un-wrap at great length the strange tale of her "twin soul," a sixty-seven-year-old Italian priest with whom she shares a magical bond that is both beautiful and very painful. As-trologers have confirmed that they are two halves of the same soul. Then we all get comfortable and on comes that new age synthesizer music as Carole Carbone tells us to relax . . . to feel a golden glow . . . to visualize ourselves at eighteen, then ten, five . . . going back . . . going back. We are in darkness, moving toward a speck of light. And we are stroll-ing into another life. A slightly eerie choir of new age voices is singing. It reminds me of the soundtrack to *The Omen*. "You're feeling very unloved," she reminds us, "and you have entered another lifetime. Be aware of the environment. Are you a male or a female? Know it now," says Carole for the first of hundreds of times. "Who is around you? Do you recognize anyone? Know it now, please." I start to panic. We are moving ahead, and I haven't found a lifetime yet. Now we, as a group, are checking out our worst decisions, we're learning important lessons, we're witnessing our own deaths. Bette Midler is tearfully singing "The Rose." And here we go, headed out for yet *another* past life, and I haven't landed a first past one yet. I feel like a complete weenie.

Later we go around the room to see how everyone has done. A blond woman is weeping because she died in 1675 and she never had a chance to tell her father she loved him. "My grandmother was my mother, and I'm like going wow," says another girl. Everywhere in the room people were marching to war or meeting their unborn children and marrying their mothers. Even my friend Carol says she thought she was an aging courtesan from another time—but then she realized what she was actually seeing was a scene from *The Last of Chéri*, by Colette, which she had just read. When we get to me, all I can do is shake my head and apologize. It's only 11:00 A.M. and already I am a failure. The best I can manage is a strange, brief scene from *Snow White and the Seven Dwarfs*. It's the part where she kisses them on their individual heads as they march off to work in the mines. So I think there's a good chance that in some other life I was Sleepy, Dopey or Grumpy. (I *know* I achieve that in this life.)

Summing up: Past life regressions average a hundred dollars per first visit. If you have that kind of money and want my opinion on what to do with it: I've been to Bermuda and had a very nice time.

THE NAKED TRUTH

I have never really figured out the whole women's underwear thing. Of course, I've worn plenty of underwear in my time—but never any expensive little teddy-and-tap-pants deals, let alone a "black lace merry widow and G-string with lightly padded underwire cups, detachable straps and garters, now specially priced."

Perhaps you've guessed that I've been receiving those exotic underwear catalogs in the mail and have been responding much as the mysterious forces that sent them had hoped I might—by giving serious thought to whether it is my duty as a woman to know how to own and operate "cami-bras" and "body-briefers."

Lingerie was never a subject of special fascination for me. I assumed that most women bought underwear the same way they bought overwear, looking for that cross-section of the reasonably cheap, the reasonably comfortable and the reasonably cute. But now I'm not so sure. "Nothing makes you feel so wonderfully pampered as silk," reads the copy for one little number that's actually larger than some of the clothes I use as my overwear. "Begin the day with the love-liest lingerie possible and see how wonderful you feel." And I'm thinking, *Leave it to me to be the only girl on my block who doesn't know how to feel wonderfully pampered. Leave it to me to be living in the underwear Dark Ages, unable to begin my day feeling as wonderful as I should.*

Continuing to berate myself for this inability to fulfill my feminine mystique, I realized that I've never really under-stood why I should buy an elaborate outfit that no one will ever see. You *are* meant to cover it with clothes, aren't you? Or are you supposed to start hanging around the house in your underwear? How do you pull off that trick without feeling like a goofball? Won't it be cold? What if the kids from the high school band come by selling mints? And most importantly, won't the man in your life come home and say, "Why are you still hanging around in your underwear?"

That would have been the response from the men I've dated, anyway. But then I've never been one of those women whom men cherish like a delicate blossom. And I assume that it's only those delicate-blossom types who understand how to make full use of underwear like this, when in *my* view, judging by the catalog photos, it was evidently created solely for giving women something seductive to wear while contemplating a single lavender rose.

During one relationship I actually bought a risqué en-semble, but I never even got to put the darned thing on because my significant other felt that the mere purchase was so out of character that it must have been one of the "Seven Deadly Warning Signs That Your Mate Is Having an Affair."

All this aside, in browsing through these catalogs I have begun to feel that dressing more provocatively would somehow make me "feel like a natural woman." Then it occurred to me that I don't actually know whether other people are playing along with all this. So I thought I'd conduct a reality check by taking the Markoe Risqué Ladies' Underwear Poll.

Methodology

I surveyed all the guys I could easily get hold of on the phone (about twenty, ranging in age from twenty-eight to forty-something). The group included a lawyer, an accountant, a high school teacher, a musician, a cameraman, a fellow who cleans pools, a model and, of course, an assortment of guys who write, produce or perform comedy for a living. There was nothing very scientific about this poll, and, furthermore, a strong case could be made that a lot of the guys I know are slightly more peculiar than normal ones. Even so, I think what they had to say is astonishing.

The Astonishing Results

I began by asking if they had ever gone to bed with a woman and found, when she disrobed, that she was wearing some exotic underwear permutation. (This is pretty much the way the fantasy scenarios in the photo layouts read—"Underneath that business suit lurks a temptress," etc.) About half of them said no. (The other half said yes.)

Then I asked what their reaction had been/would be in the event of such a thing. About half said they had enjoyed or would enjoy it. That much I expected. But fully half said they would find it off-putting, even a little scary. "It would be like 'Uh-oh, what have I gotten myself into?' " said a big, strong, handsome producer. "Like, what does she mean by this?" said a writer who is just as big, strong and handsome. "Kind of like 'Who's taking advantage of whom here?' " said the accountant. "It could be positive or negative," said the high school teacher, "but I'd figure she'd really been around."

The following fact was even more surprising: All but four of the men said they feel uncomfortable when confronted, in public, with a provocatively dressed woman, i.e., someone in a short, tight dress that reveals a lot of cleavage.

One guy said he couldn't "have a relationship with a woman who was trying to attract other men's eyes." Another said that he prejudges women dressed in an overtly sexual manner as "probably not very intelligent."

Then two of the guys said this look would be okay if the woman approached it with a sense of humor—"like kind of a spoof." Several said that if they picked up a woman on a date and she was wearing a sexually aggressive outfit they would feel uncomfortable enough to talk to her about it. And, I reiterate, these were big, strong, handsome guys to whom I was speaking.

I was amazed! I've always thought that most women (and this includes, at least, me) believe that men would like them to dress as seductively as possible, as often as possible. And where would we get such an idea? From advertising, TV and movies that are plastered with women dressed provocatively and that are, for the most part, brought to us by men. And then, by observing those men with whom we have contact in real life staring at color photos of these alluring ensembles, openmouthed and dazed, looking as if they've been hit on the head with a mallet . . .

Don't tell me that women, all on their own, came up with the idea of wearing twenty-five pounds of boning, wiring, buckles, straps and hydraulic equipment under their clothes. While we must have agreed to it, we definitely did it to please men. They must have *told* us they liked it at the time.

In wrapping up my poll, I asked the guys what they think *does* constitute sexy clothing. A couple said they don't much care, that it was the woman herself they found sexy. One said, "Summer dresses." Another said, "Tailored clothing that really fits right." A third man came up with "an oversize T-shirt." A fourth seemed to sum it all up when he said, "Clothing that isn't intended to seem sexy. Like maybe a ripped sweatshirt or an outfit you'd paint the house in."

So the results turned out to be kind of sweet and endearing, particularly to me, since I already own ripped sweatshirts in a wide variety of colors. And whether or not this group accurately reflects the rest of society, I'm just glad to have found out how my friends feel before making the wrong choice some Halloween and causing a lot of them premature heart failure.

FIRING MY DOG

The recession is something that affects each American differently. But as I sat staring it in the face, it occurred to me that there were some obvious ways to cut my expenses dramatically. Which is why, one day in late summer, I called for my new dog Lewis to come in to my office. Since he never comes when I call him, I finally gave up and succeeded in locating him out in the yard underneath a hedge, where I was able to make him stop digging and look me in the eye.

Me: Lewis . . .

Lewis: Help me pull these impatiens out of the ground.

Me: No. Stop that. Leave those shrubs alone.

Lewis: Just take part of this in your mouth and pull on it. I think it is almost loose enough to uproot.

Me: No! Stop it! No! This is exactly what I wanted to talk to you about. I realize you're just out of puppyhood and all, but you are very destructive, very poorly behaved and you are costing me an incredible amount of money.

Lewis: Well, this has been fascinating but sorry, I can't stay. You don't expect me to sit here and destroy just this one plant all afternoon.

Me: Lewis. Listen to me. I've been going through my financial records and it comes to my attention that I've been spending several hundred dollars per month on you, minimum. And to be frank, I'm having a great deal of difficulty justifying that kind of financial outlay.

Lewis: Cost of living increases. Services rendered. Do I have to itemize them for you?

Me: Services rendered? Yes, do that. Go ahead and itemize them for me. *What services rendered?*

Lewis: Well, for example, shrub removal runs you eight bucks an hour. It's demanding work.

Me: You mean you're *charging* me for ruining my yard? I already pay a bunch of guys from El Salvador to do that.

Lewis: They're not thorough. I gotta move. Come with me. It'll save you money. You know, sitting here at your feet goes for six bucks an hour.

Me: Am I hearing correctly? You charge me to sit at my feet?

Lewis: Of course I charge you. You see anyone else sitting at your feet voluntarily?

Me: I'm stunned. What else do you charge for?

Lewis: Room-to-room barking. You don't get a service like that for nothing. Ball's got a ten-buck-an-hour one-hour minimum.

Me: I can't get over this. You *charge* me to play ball? I thought you *liked* ball.

Lewis: Guess again. And it's seventy-five bucks an hour to sleep on the bed with you.

Me: Are you serious? You mean I am *paying* you to cover my bed with grime and bugs and hair? What *are* those little hard chunks anyway?

Lewis: Don't worry about those. I throw those in at cost.

Me: You know something, I am *glad* we had this little talk because these are all services I can live without. Plus, you destroy my books. You eat my hats and my shoes. You broke into my closet and ate my souvenir collection.

Lewis: I'm sure there was a work order issued on that. I went into golden time that day. It's dangerous to eat souvenirs. God only knows what they're made of.

Me: Well, that's the last straw. I've heard enough. I'm going to have to let you go. You're fired.

Lewis: You can't just fire me. I have a contract.

Me: Get out.

Lewis: You're looking at a lawsuit, lady.

Me: Fine. Sue me. Get out.

Lewis: I'm not going anywhere. Go ahead. Try and move me. Did you ever try to lift a six-hundred-pound sack of lawn clippings? You aren't going to be able to budge me. I've seen you struggling with the bottled-water refills. And even if you do get me out the front door, I'm just going to stand there and whine and bark ceaselessly until all your neighbors get pissed off at you. Believe me, I'm going *no-where*. In fact, unless you want to apologize, I might start the barking right now. . . .

....

What the Dogs Have Taught Me

Me: No, no. Wait. Don't start barking. . . .

Lewis: Here I go. I don't hear an apology.

Me: Wait, wait. You're on probation. Okay, okay. . . . I'm sorry.

Lewis: By the way, "no barking" is three bucks a minute.

A WORLD
WITHOUT MEN

*A couple of weeks ago I attended an inven-*tors' convention at the Pasadena Center Exhibition Building, a large hall crammed with exhibitor's booths, in which the proud mothers of new inventions were showing off their bright ideas. What struck me about the affair was that the overwhelming majority of these mothers were men.

The inventions were addressed to a wide range of humanity's needs, but one of the most popular categories turned out to be (for reasons I still haven't got a bead on) variations on the toilet. There were two types of "odorless" toilets, one involving filters and one involving vacuums and air fresheners. There was a portable traveler's toilet, a "multi-user entertainment system super top" toilet and a toilet-seat alarm system that was activated whenever anyone forgot to put the seat back down. And even *that* was invented by a man.

Another man, named Sergio Regalado, was at the convention trying to mass-market an idea that he claimed was popular in the eighteenth and nineteenth centuries: the tongue scraper. "If you never scrape your tongue, you'll always have bad breath," he vigorously explained, causing a thoughtful listener to shudder at the thought of a minimum of two centuries' worth of horrible breath we've all had to endure. Perhaps the goofiest new take on the whole better-health thing came from a scientist and engineer called Dr. Edward Richards, who, in addition to having invented some canoe-shaped, wheel-laden airplane-landing-gear deal, had also brought along the plans and prototypes for the "medical muffler device," which, says the press release, "allows gas from the gastrointestinal tract to escape slowly, silently, continually and odorless." "My grandchild had a problem with the gas release," he explained to me in a deadly somber Slavic accent of some kind, "and it was hell for everyone." And thus was born an invention.

On the drive home I found myself wondering why it was that so few women had seen fit to contribute to an event such as this. To be fair, there *had* been a couple. Offhand, I could think of two I had seen. Both had invented new types of dolls. This, as compared with one wild-eyed man who had bothered to reinvent the alphabet and intended to try and push it forward until every single piece of printed material in the world had been redone to his specifications. The explanation I came up with for the paucity of female crackpot inventors was that they probably had something better to do. Women just didn't want to bother inventing a toilet-seat alarm when they already had devises such as yelling, pouting and brooding resentfully in pretty good working order. As for the grandchild's problem with the gas release, I don't think a woman would have felt the need for a peculiar plastic muffler deal if she knew that the bran muffin had already been invented.

As I continued to conjecture along these lines, I began to construct my own crackpot theory with regard to the essential nature of the sexes. My theory is that the very structure of daily life on the planet would have been totally different if there had never been men, since men think so extremely differently from women. To illustrate this, I have compiled a short list of things I feel would never have existed at all had there never been any men.

MEALTIMES. Women might have toyed with the idea of sitting down to big plates of several kinds of food three times a day but almost certainly would have rejected it right away because it was so fattening. Instead they would have opted for a few spoons of cottage cheese at 10:30 A.M., an apple at noon, a couple of bites of chocolate-chip cookie at three, forkfuls of whatever someone nearby was eating at around five, and then random nibbling up until bedtime. This syndrome also makes men the rightful heirs to the TV dinner, as I have never met a woman who cared about having a small amount of peas and a tablespoon of mashed potatoes with her Salisbury steak.

PROJECTILE WEAPONRY. I don't think women would have come up with guns. Maybe not even bows and arrows. In their quest for food, I think, women would have developed concepts along the lines of fly-fishing, wherein one makes little miniatures of the diet of the intended prey to trick it with. But then we might have ended up liking the little miniatures so much that we would keep them for accessories or collectibles, rationalizing that, after all, a handful of grass or berries would be a lot less effort than fish, a lot fewer calories than another plate of greasy ground squirrel.

ALL THOSE DIFFERENT SPORTS INVOLVING ALL THOSE DIFFERENT KINDS OF BALLS. Women would have invented one, at most two, really good ones—volleyball and soccer, let's say—and then, figuring that two seemed like plenty, probably would have plowed ahead and developed a multitude of hair-care products. Men, on the other hand, almost definitely would have called it a game after the invention of *one* shampoo, never even bothering to write up the concepts for creme rinses, finishing rinses or extra-body conditioners, let alone styling gels and mousses.

VARIOUS FORMS OF ENTERTAINMENT INVOLVING CAR EXPLOSIONS. This category includes TV, movies, races, Grand Prix and toys that simulate all of the above. I would venture to say that if there had been no men, there almost certainly would not have been any nitro-burning funny cars. In fact, when you consider how enamored women have traditionally been of horses, it makes you wonder if cars would have been invented at all.

ARMIES. I don't see women dreaming up a highly disciplined, drably outfitted, ordeal-oriented, well-oiled fighting machine. Nah. I also don't think women would have bothered with long-range missile systems—especially after we had worked out all the details of other systems, such as slapping and scratching.

VCRs. Since women have so much trouble operating them, I am going to assume that we wouldn't have bothered with them at all.

All of the above are clear-cut examples of the distinctive approach to logical thought that is unique to men. Of course, this extends into behavior, too. Take interior decoration. I don't think the woman has been born to whom it would occur to substitute sports equipment lined up next to the wall for furniture groupings and area rugs. And yet I have frequently visited the "home" of a man who thought this was a fine idea.

It is thought processes like these that eventually find creative release in the invention of tongue scrapers and multi-user entertainment-system toilet-tank tops. Not to mention telephone systems, stereo equipment and electric carving knives. Those darn men, God bless 'em.

CONVERSATION PIECE

I recently spent one of those weeks where I hardly spoke a word out loud. This is the sort of life experience that is almost totally unimaginable in New York City, where one's proximity to complete strangers causes a regular number of pointless verbal exchanges. I call them verbal exchanges because I don't think "I was here first" "Well, what do you want? A medal?" can be classified as a conversation per se.

I have been giving some serious thought to the nature of conversation (as serious as I am capable of) just in case I ever have one again.

First, it is important to note that men and women regard conversation quite differently. For women it is a passion, a sport, an activity even more important to life than eating because it doesn't involve weight gain. The first sign of closeness among women is when they find themselves engaging in endless, secretless rounds of conversation with one another. And as soon as a woman begins to relax and feel comfortable in a relationship with a man, she tries to have that type of conversation with him as well. However, the first sign that a man is feeling close to a woman is when he admits that he'd rather she please quiet down so he can hear the TV. A man who feels truly intimate with a woman often reserves for her and her alone the precious gift of one-word answers. Everyone knows that the surest way to spot a successful long-term relationship is to look around a restaurant for the table where no one is talking. Ah . . . now *that's* real love.

But to get to that blissful state, the relationship usually passes through a conversational stage first, which is why I thought I'd take this opportunity to present:

The Merrill Markoe Course in Conversation

WHAT IS A CONVERSATION? For our purposes, it is any exchange of more than two remarks that does not end in an act of violence. The successful conversationalist always remembers to first remove all extraneous objects from the mouth (and hide them, unless you are prepared to make that the topic of the conversation, and quite frankly I have found that admitting "I just *like* the feel of packing materials between my teeth and I don't really care that they're made of toxic chemicals" is not the sort of opening remark that shows one off in the best light).

Always remember to ENUNCIATE clearly. If you notice that the person to whom you are talking is reacting with a blank stare, repeat the phrases "Can you hear me?" and "Do you understand?" in louder and louder tones of voice until you ascertain that your conversational partner (a) does not have a language in common with you, or (b) is in some kind of a stupor. (The former condition is more frequent on the East Coast, the latter on the West. Either situation renders the whole thing pretty hopeless and gives you permission to call a cab.) Which brings us to another basic point: Remember that the creation of new language is the sole domain of advertising copywriters and desperate Scrabble players. And that the words created by these people, such as *Scrum-diddly-umptious*, *FUNtastic* and *CHOC-o-licious*—or, in the case of Scrabble, *zziquox*—should never be spoken aloud, even in the privacy of your own home.

Now that we have discussed form, let's move ahead to content.

An important part of any successful conversation is, of course, a good OPENING REMARK, one that is designed to intrigue, inspire and delight. Which is why "Leave me alone," "Please leave me alone" and "Won't you please, please leave me alone" are not good opening remarks. Oddly enough, the opposite—as in "Please, I beg of you, talk to me!"—does not work either. It is considered a turnoff by many. The best opening remark, therefore, is on the surface cheering and neutral but contains an essentially truthful subtext that says, "Do you have the time to listen to me drone on ceaselessly about my problems for as long as I find it convenient?" Examples of this type of opening remark are "Hi. How are you? You look great. That's a very nice purse. Where'd you get it?" and "Hey, what's happening?"

Okay! Now that we've got the old conversational ball rolling, your next important task is to figure out SOMETHING TO SAY. If you have nothing to say but still feel the need simply to hear yourself talk—maybe just for the facial exercise, or to prove that you're alive—then the appropriate outlet is, of course, talk radio, where a handsomely paid professional moderator is willing to pretend to care about your views on Barbara Bush's weight or the inflated salaries of professional athletes.

"But," you may say to me, "Merrill, Merrill, Merrill. . . . What if I see someone I barely know and want to talk to them? Then what?" And I would say back to you, "First, don't ever use my name three times in a row like that. It puts you well over the legal lifetime limit for using my first name in a sentence." And then I would have to say that this is the best time to use:

The Merrill Markoe Sociological Stereotyping Chart

Clever sociological stereotyping can help you make the sweeping generalizations that are useful conversation starters. Or they will get you a punch in the mouth. Either way you have had that important initial contact with the person of your choice. What I am referring to is the fact that certain types of people are more likely to be interested in certain topics. For example, if you choose "Methods of Scoring Hockey" as your topic of conversation with the average middle-class woman, you're probably making a bad choice. Which is not to say that the average middle-class woman for whom this is a passionate topic does not exist. (Okay.

The woman does not exist.) But just as the average middle-class man does not like to talk about his emotions or anything of importance *except* methods of scoring hockey, there is a reason why hockey scoring is the only topic never addressed by Geraldo, Oprah, Phil and Sally Jessy Raphael.

Presented below is a short reference chart indicating some topics and the corresponding demographic sampling that may find them interesting. You will probably want to make up your own list. Or maybe not, if you have any kind of a real life.

Topic	Who Will Talk About It
What we as individuals can do to make this planet called Earth a better place to live	Students under the age of twenty-five and sit-com stars who are not getting enough media attention
The plots of highly rated network TV shows such as *Who's the Boss?* and *Full House*	No one. Being forced to listen to this is considered grounds for justifiable homicide in eighteen states
How they score televised sports	Men between the ages of twenty-five and sixty
Why the men in their life won't talk about anything but televised sports	Women between the ages of eighteen and seventy

Topic	Who Will Talk About It
The weather	Employees of dry-cleaning establishments or the U.S. Postal Service; your parents or, if they're not home, my parents
The deteriorating health of people you barely know	Your mother or, if she's not home, my mother
What it means that all your man will talk about is sports and all your parents will talk about is the weather and the deteriorating health of people you barely know	Mental health professionals; me

All righty, now that you have successfully initiated the conversation, another problem is likely to present itself. More and more it seems as though a person (and of course by "a person" I mean "me") runs into someone who tells the same story over and over, beat for beat. They never even bother to say, "Stop me if you've heard this one before" and do not feel the least bit deterred when they notice that you are mouthing along with them as though you were an audience member at a sing-along. What do you do?

I recommend an exercise that I call CREATIVE CONVER-

SATIONAL VISUALIZATION. As the person drones on, imagine that he is being squashed flat as a bug by a giant steamroller. Now, as you gaze downward at a two-dimensional aerial view of your formerly three-dimensional friend, see if you can answer the following questions: Would he make an interesting piece of abstract art? What sort of frame would you buy for it, and where would you hang it in your home? And, while you're at it, how much do you think you could get for the piece at an art auction? While you proceed with the answers to these questions, do not forget to meet the traditional obligation of "Mmm hmm" and "I see" at five-second intervals.

"But Merrill," you say to me (and of course when I say "you" I mean "me"), "what do I do if I continue to be trapped, a virtual prisoner of dull conversation that threatens to go on until the end of time? Then what?" This is the proper moment for a polite but firm remark that allows you to exit quickly, one that does not hurt the feelings of your conversational partner, such as, "I see by my oxygen sensor that there is not enough breathable air on this part of the planet, and since one of us is in danger, I will make the sacrifice and leave." Then you turn on your heel and run like the wind—after, of course, waving a polite good-bye.

MADONNA AND CARRIE VS. MERRILL AND ELAYNE

Recently I began to worry about the fact that I was the only remaining columnist in America who hadn't written about Madonna. Then her movie came out, followed by even *more* interviews and articles, and I started to grow concerned that there was just nothing left to be said about her. And this was *before* the big two-part piece in *Rolling Stone* where Madonna sat down with Carrie Fisher and they discussed every remaining thing that either of them had neglected to mention in the multitude of lengthy in-depth interviews each of them had given previously. Now I was truly frightened. But what could I do? It *is* a California state law that *everyone* with access to a publisher *must* turn in at least *one* piece about Madonna by the end of this fiscal year. So with time running out, I invited my friend Elayne Boosler over to help me reflect on the Madonna–Carrie Fisher confab. She arrived with a bottle of champagne and her dog

Petey, who immediately developed a perverse attraction to my dog Lewis which never let up for one second of the five hours we all hung out.

Elayne: Well, they begin the article by mentioning that they both go to the same shrink. You tried to get me to go to your shrink for many years.

Merrill: I actually *did* go to one of your shrinks once. Between us we've seen quite a few shrinks. I don't know if either of us went to their shrink.

E: They mention that they're each competing to be the best or worst patient their shrink has. I'm guessing they've achieved that. They want to impress their shrink. I want to impress my dry cleaner.

M: What can you do to impress your dry cleaner?

E: I bring in extremely clean clothing. I get it cleaned first.

M: See, I go the opposite way. I try for really spectacular stains. To give the impression I lead a fast, dangerous life. You have to be the best customer or the worst customer.

E: I'm the best.

M: I'm the worst.

E: My dry cleaner is the only person I gave my picture to because he meets me at airports with clean clothes when I'm on tour. But I think he should put up pictures of doctors, lawyers, Ralph Nader, guys who know quality. Who would take the recommendation of a comedian?

M: Oddly enough, Carrie Fisher and Madonna don't even touch on this subject.

E: I bet their shrink does their cleaning. They probably pay $500 an hour. For that I think you also get your pants pressed.

M: Now they get to the fact that they've both been married and divorced.

E: We haven't.

M: We all have famous exes. But I don't think we want to talk about that.

E: No. Madonna's nickname is tattooed on Sean Penn's toe. Have you ever had a man tattoo your name anywhere?

M: Well, they all *wanted* to but I always talked them down. Do you even have a nickname?

E: No. I had one guy who called me Pumpkin. I said, "Do you call all your girlfriends Pumpkin?" He said, "Just the last six." I don't think Jews *have* nicknames.

M: Carrie Fisher is a mixed breed but I guess you don't need a nickname when your name is Carrie. It would have to be longer and more formal. Like Carlisle.

E: I never thought of Eddie Fisher as Jewish because he married a woman who was wearing so much makeup and who was going to get fat later. Actually, that *is* very Jewish.

M: You mean Elizabeth Taylor? I think my father would have left my mother for Elizabeth Taylor. So we have that in common. I would like to note at this point that your dog Petey has been having what I'll refer to as air-sex with my dog Lewis pretty much nonstop.

E: And now he's having it with himself. He's the only guy who takes "Go fuck yourself" so literally. I remember when I was a kid there was a picture of Elizabeth Taylor on the cover of *Life* magazine on her fortieth or fiftieth birthday. How old is she now? Ninety?

M: Just under eighty. She's seventy-eight.

E: She supposedly had just come out of the shower and was

wearing no makeup so we know how long this took. Five hours of six makeup artists going, "It'll be very natural."

M: And then they get the sand blaster out.

E: She was wearing just two purple towels. One on her head, and one on her breasts. . . .

M: And just a hint of anesthetic behind each ear to dull the pain from the surgery.

E: They were actually doing a live liposuction on her during the picture. They had live men sucking the fat out of her and my father says, "Look at this! The most beautyful woman in the world! She's forty or fifty and she doesn't need to wear a stitch of makeup." I was two years old and I said, "You idiot. You think this woman has no makeup on?" Now we get to the part where they learn they have Warren in common.

M: Did you fuck Warren?

E: Oh, sure. Who hasn't?

M: It's a city ordinance. I wanted to be his best patient.

E: Carrie says, "I was seventeen and making *Shampoo.*" That probably means she was twenty-five.

M: She made shampoo? From scratch? That's very young to know how to make shampoo. I've made toothpaste with baking soda but I wonder where she learned to make shampoo?

E: She didn't make it herself. It says she made it with Warren Beatty.

M: Bad reality. Good anecdote. They say that a lot in here.

E: It's a very writerly thing to say.

M: Do you get many anecdotes out of bad reality?

E: No. I work mainly with okay reality and try to make it really interesting.

M: Me, too. I don't like to talk about bad reality. It's too painful. I think the weirdness of everyday bland reality is my specialty. Now here they talk about how they both have hostility toward men.

E: We don't. We let them step on us but then we try and trip them on their way out.

M: And later we talk about them. I guess I never thought of Madonna as being hostile toward men.

E: Well, do you put your tits in a pencil sharpener when you go to work?

M: Madonna says she likes to shock but not offend.

E: I like to shop but not offend.

M: I think she shocks and offends. I keep trying to like her but she keeps pissing me off.

E: Well, here Carrie Fisher points out that she uses a lot of crass language. Like in her movie talking about being finger fucked by a girl from her high school.

M: Why do you suppose she wants everyone to know that about her? This is what I always call "the curse of too much information." Why would anyone want everyone to know all this really personal stuff about them?

E: I think it's about feeling desperate. Some people don't exist unless someone is looking. Or the other reason is you're trying to get a mortgage. Then they have to know everything. Including who you finger fucked. Maybe she was buying a house.

What the Dogs Have Taught Me

Part Two

M: I'm just going to designate this part two, if that's okay.

E: Fine.

M: My point is that both of us use our lives in our work but we both edit and censor heavily.

E: This guy who made Madonna's film observed her every day for seven months. I have my picture taken, and in two minutes I'm saying "Hurry. Hurry." Well! Here Madonna uses the word "assuage." I'm extremely impressed. It almost makes up for some of the crude stuff. Although she might have said "assauge." This we don't know. My guess is she said "assauge."

M: She also says "epiglottis" somewhere in there.

E: She does not!

M: I guess she's not a dumb girl.

E: I guess you didn't see that *Nightline* interview. You know, if we only had a video cam the dogs could be on Bob Saget's show and we could win like a million dollars and not have to do any of this. Petey! Enough!

M: I can't believe they aren't worn out yet.

E: Why can't we find guys like this? I sat next to Madonna at a Laura Nyro concert and she was further from her stage persona than anyone I've ever seen. She looked so different it was unbelievable.

M: Did Madonna know who you were?

E: No. But McDonald's knows who I am. It says here that Madonna went to a seder and got drunk because she was out of her element. We would get drunk because we were with our families.

M: Too far into our element.

E: You know, now on Passover a lot of people who used to leave a chair for Elijah leave a chair for Madonna. They figure it's the same odds.

M: The odds would be better if they left two chairs. Elijah might show up sooner if he thought he'd be sitting next to Madonna. Have you ever met Carrie Fisher?

E: No. But I once sang a duet with Eddie Fisher. On the Perry Como show. (*She begins to sing*) "Oh! My Papa! To me he was so wonderful!"

M: It's nice watching dogs hump to that song. I feel I finally understand it.

E (*singing*)*:* "Oh! My Papa! To me he was so grand."

M: Gees, what a weird song that was. Like a funeral dirge.

E: Have you ever heard "My Yiddishe Mama"? Talk about a sad song. (*She sings*) "My Yiddishe Mama. I miss her more than ever now. My Yiddishe Mama. I long to kiss that furrowed brow."

M: The dogs are really banging away to this one.

E: That's how it's used these days. To get animals to mate faster on farms.

M: I think Jews stopped writing songs like those once therapy was invented. In fact, I think songs like those are *why* therapy was invented. Madonna says when she first heard the word "penis" she was horrified.

E: I was wondering lately what chance women have for happiness when you consider that two thirds of the word "happiness" is "penis."

M: I think, before we close, we should take a little time to discuss blow jobs since that, for me, was the most startling and amazing part of the Carrie Fisher and Madonna discussion. Where Madonna came out against them. Do you have anything to say about them?

E: No.

M: Well, with that I think we've covered everything. At least I pray we have.

Evolution of the Species. Not.

If the Universe is a High School (and you'll have to be polite and play along with the metaphor for this next part to work), then our culture is definitely the eighth grade. It's run by eighth-grade boys, and the way these boys show a girl they like her is by humiliating her and making her cry. Every time a perfect example of this behavior erupts in public I am quietly pleased, because it proves to me that I am not just a bitter malcontent who's making all this up as a way of explaining away my own shortcomings.

Lately it seems to me that everywhere I look the eighth-grade boys are standing on their desks and shooting spitballs. In politics! In show business! In savings-and-loan problems and the N.E.A. thing. It's everywhere! It's nationwide. It's coast-to-coast! It's so completely out of control that you'd think there was a substitute president in charge.

Of course the most vivid recent example was the Anita

Hill–Clarence Thomas brouhaha. This was absolutely the Eighth Grade Student Council in full session. So okay, like here's what happened:

There was this girl in the class named Anita Hill who was kind of pretty and kind of a brain so a lot of the boys didn't really like her because they thought that *she* thought she was so smart and everything. Except this one guy, Clarence Thomas, who sat next to her in English and math— he was like the President of the Chess Club, and the Representative from Liberia at the Model U.N. and everything, except he was like this really uptight straight guy because he was one of the only black guys at the school so I guess he wanted to be in with the white guys but he never could be exactly? Even when he stopped wearing such dorky shoes. I mean like he tried *really really* hard all the time and always got straight A's and came to school in a suit and a tie and everything? Except that not many people really liked him because he was so uptight that you could never really know how he felt about things so he wasn't very much fun or anything. Anyway, he kept asking Anita Hill out and she would never really go out with him. And this really bugged him because he thought she thought she was *so* big. So he like started trying to get her attention by telling her about all these really dirty movies that he supposedly saw. He probably thought that would make her think he was not such a complete nerd or something but instead it only grossed her out more and she didn't know what to do or anything. So she told her Mom about it and her Mom told her, "Ignore him and he'll stop," only he didn't? He kept getting worse and worse and told even grosser and grosser stories and the more she got grossed out the bigger a brat he became? I don't know what he thought he was accomplishing but the thing about a lot of the eighth-grade boys is that they don't know what they're doing but they go ahead and do it anyway? *Especially* if it bugs you.

So anyhow, eventually she got so bugged by him that she figured out a way to get transferred to another homeroom. I don't know what he did then, probably found another girl to bug or something like that. And everything was cool until Anita heard that Clarence was running for Student Council President and then she had to go "Yick!!!" So she starts in telling her friends about the really gross stuff he said and they all agree that she should rat on him at assembly. Because maybe if more people knew, they wouldn't want a gross guy like that to represent them?

So after a while, a lot of the eighth-grade girls were on her side. They were like all prepared to get up and give speeches and everything—until they saw all the boys get on stage at the assembly and realized something they had known all along but had also kind of forgotten, which was that the Student Council was almost 100 percent eighth-grade boys?

And then when the smart girls got up to give their speeches the boys wouldn't shut up and pay attention or anything. It didn't even matter that the girls wrote really good speeches and got dressed up and looked really cute and all because the eighth-grade boys on the Student Council secretly thought they had cooties anyway.

So suddenly it's like really weird. The smart girls are saying this stuff and not only is no one listening but then who do they let get up and speak for about a million hours but—can you believe it?—*John Doggett?* Only the biggest brat and nerd in the entire class. I mean, John Doggett is like one of those guys you wouldn't even dance with if he asked you because he dances so creepy but doesn't even know it? I mean, he couldn't even get elected to the Student Council if he tried, but now he gets to get up and say all this stuff which he thinks makes him seem like he's "in" with those guys and one of them and everything. And here he is getting up to give a speech about how Anita Hill really liked him but he didn't like her? *Not.* Like she couldn't even remember who he was!!! And she says so and everything, but suddenly all the eighth-grade boys decide they're going to listen to *him* for once in their lives because of course he's on their side and he's a guy and everything. And he's all stoked because he probably thinks that now they're going to invite him to their parties and to hang out with them on weekends and stuff. *Not.*

That's how it all sounded to me. Eighth grade run amok from start to finish. And for years and years I've been pretending this kind of thing didn't bother me just because I didn't want to sound strident and whiney. But now I can't stop thinking about it.

Show business, to give another example, is eighth-grade-boys' P.E. With the Thomas-Hill hearings on my mind, I was stalking around the video rental place the other night, looking for movies to take home. It kept occurring to me that most of the so-called mainstream movies are made for eighth-grade boys—the whole Simpson-Bruckheimer-drive-a - cool - new - super - fast - vehicle - through - exploding - plate - glass-windows genre.

As a guy who habitually wears hightop basketball shoes in his sleek corner office explained to me last week, no women are really considered "box office" these days. And he meant in mainstream movies, the ones that occupy the "new movie" shelves at the video rental place. And just what is it that occupies these shelves? *Whole rows* of movies that seem to have been made for boys only. I'm referring to the films of people like Steven Seagal, Jean-Claude Van Damme and Chuck Norris.

I'd known about them for years but never even considered going to see one in an actual movie theater. This time, as I stared at the cover photos on the cassettes, featuring muscular, scowling eighth-grade guys in aggressive poses, I remembered that I have been known to *like* eighth-grade boys now and then, especially the cute ones. Maybe these movies had something for a gal like me. Was there enough moistened, hunkering sinew here to be titillating? Or were they exclusively flying fists and feet and blazing fire power? Were they just for boys? I wondered.

After watching seven of these movies, one after another, I can definitely answer, "Yes. They're for boys only." And not even eighth-grade boys in the case of Chuck Norris, whose films have obviously been made by the fourth-grade boys who follow the eighth-grade boys around, awestruck. These movies remind me of nothing so much as the drawings that little boys do of squadrons of nasty-looking aircraft unleashing torrents of bombs and causing millions of explosions. A random scanning of *Delta Force II* revealed that at almost any point in the dialogue you'll hear, "Colonel Cooper. The preparations have begun on the C-100s at 0700 hours."

Then there's Steven Seagal, a man whose lima-bean head/earring/ponytail combination give him the look of a record promoter with a character disorder. His signature involves snapping at least one arm and one leg in half during big fight sequences—whether he's playing Mason Storm, a renegade cop in a fancy suit who watched while his wife was brutally slain by drug lords, or John Hatcher, a renegade ex-cop in a sport coat with rolled-up sleeves who watched as his sister was almost brutally slain by drug lords.

Which brings us neatly to the role that women occupy in all of these films, one that is eerily reminiscent of the role adorable housepets play when they are introduced early in the story line of movies like *Nightmare on Elm Street*. They are there to be killed and then, in death, to serve as a justifiable motive for the rage and mayhem of the eighth-grade hero. At the precise moment that an emotional tie begins to form between a woman and anyone else, we know the countdown to her checkout time has begun.

To look on the bright side of Steven Seagal (which, I believe, is the side with the earring), his sense of himself as a ladies' man does require him to have human females in his movies—even if they are nude or dead or both. Jean-Claude Van Damme, the only one of the bunch with sex appeal, also has the occasional love interest but seems to prefer pining for an unattainable object of desire. In *Death Warrant*, in which he goes undercover in a prison with a 99 percent male cast, visiting rules keep him down to one quickly interrupted, almost-passionate kiss with his lady lawyer. As he says to a fellow prisoner who has the wrong idea about him, "I don't pay. I don't ponk." (At least that's as close as I could come to deciphering it.)

So where, I wearily ask, are the movies for girls? And what would they contain if there were any?

I think it's kind of telling that boys' movies envision a world that has few women or none at all. I can't imagine women turning out for a film that promised them "Not a man as far as the eye can see." Maybe the fact that they're in our fantasies but we're not in theirs is part of the problem.

I read recently in the *Los Angeles Times* that among Japanese cognoscenti there is a deepening contempt for American culture. Akiyuki Nosaka, a famous Japanese novelist, is quoted as saying that "Looking at the United States is like watching a test run for the decline of the human race." I have to admit that lately this kind of thought has been haunting me, too. And I think that the eighth-grade boys' uninterrupted reign of terror is the root of all the trouble. I don't know how this can be reversed, but I secretly believe that women would like to graduate and that it's just the really bad attitude of a bunch of the eighth-grade boys that's holding back the rest of the class.

WHAT THE DOGS HAVE TAUGHT ME

Daily Routine

The day is divided into two important sections. *Mealtime*. And *everything else*.

I. MEALTIME

1. Just because there does not seem to be anything *visible* around to eat certainly does not mean there is *nothing* around to eat. The act of staring at the underside of a table or chair on which someone else is eating sets in motion a chain of events that eventually results in food.

2. It goes without saying that you should carefully check the lower third of *any* space for edibles. Mouth-sized things which cannot be identified by sight or smell are considered gum.

3. When you actually receive a meal, submerge your head into it as you would a shower. *Never, ever* look up again until a minimum of at least fifteen minutes after the obvious food is gone. This is important. Just because your dish is empty does not mean that it is time to stop eating.

4. Remember that *all* food is potentially yours up until the time that it is actually swallowed by another. The lengthy path a piece of food will take from a plate to a mouth via a hand is as good a time as any to stake your claim to it.

5. When it comes to selecting an appropriate beverage, location and packaging mean *nothing*. There are *absolutely no exceptions* to this rule.

6. If you really see something you want, and all your other attempts at getting it have failed, it is only right to grovel shamelessly. As a second tactic, stare intently at the object of your desire, allowing long gelatinous drools to leak like icicles from your lower lip.

II. EVERYTHING ELSE

1. There are really only two important facial expressions to bother with: *complete overwhelming joy* and *nothing at all*.

2. Any time that is not meal time is potentially nap time. The best time to take a nap is when you hear your name being called repeatedly. The best location for a nap is dead center of any street or driveway. The most relaxing position is on your side, all four limbs parallel.

3. The most practical way to get dry is to shake violently near a fully clothed person. A second effective method is to stand on a light-colored piece of furniture.

4. *Personal Security*

　　A. At the first hint of any irregular noise, run from

room to room yelling loudly. If someone actually comes into the house, rush over to them whether you know them or not. Then kiss them so violently that they lose their balance or have to force you away physically.

B. The greatest unacknowledged threat to life as we have come to know it is squirrels. No matter what you must do, make sure there are none in your yard.

5. *Recreation and Leisure*

A. *Ball:* There are two equally amusing sets of rules you will want to know.

   a. *The common form,* in which you receive a thrown ball and return it.

   b. *The preferred form,* in which you receive a thrown ball and eat it.

B. *Car:* As you know, any open car door is an invitation to get in. Once inside, your only goal is to try to get out.

6. *Health*

A. In the event of a trip to the doctor, always be on your guard. If you are vaccinated, urinate on the physician.

Afterword

Since I have taken to sleeping under the bed, I have come to know tranquility I never imagined possible.

You never really know when it might be cookie time. And that's what the dogs have taught me.

....